Simple Steps to Green Meetings and Events

The Professional's Guide to Saving Money and the Earth

Amy Spatrisano, CMP & Nancy J. Wilson, CMP

Printed in the United States of America.

This book is printed on recycled paper that contains 100% post-consumer fiber.

Cataloguing-in-Publication data is available from the Library of Congress.
ISBN: 987-0-615-16990-3

Table of Contents

Foreward

Though we've been called pioneers and trailblazers for green meetings, we are not the original pioneers. The concept of green meetings has been around since the late 1980s and early 1990s. The perspective back then was to green your meetings because "it's the right thing to do" for the environment. The challenge with that perspective is that it was not sustainable. Although we believe people really do want to do "the right thing," incorporating that approach into business just didn't sell. The economic bottom line was the driving motivation.

In our first presentation about green meetings we realized going in that it wasn't enough just to talk about the environmental merits of going green. Fortuitously, we attended a Natural Step Framework workshop about sustainability and learned how to develop a business case. It became clear that what was missing from the conversation about green meetings was the business case. So we began our journey to create the business case for green meetings. We began by collecting data that illustrated cost savings, showed examples of how green meetings offered a competitive advantage, and discussed how impending regulation would begin to affect how meeting services were conducted.

It's taken more than six years of continued refinement and data collection to strengthen the business case. We never gave up talking about green meetings and explaining the business case even in the face of unresponsive crowds, chiding from colleagues and the continued disinterest of the industry at large. All this changed in 2007, when there seemed to be the development of a perfect storm. Al Gore's film "An Inconvenient Truth" won an Academy Award, New Orleans was still reeling from the devastation of hurricane Katrina, more and more regions were experiencing their own unusual and harsh weather conditions, and every magazine from Newsweek to Sports Illustrated had cover stories addressing sustainability. Suddenly the world was paying attention – including the meetings industry.

The floodgates have opened, and more and more meeting professionals are realizing they need to be educated about sustainability and learn how to respond to the growing demand for green meetings. We realized it was time to finish and publish this book to provide you with the tools to do just that.

We are grateful for the original pioneers who forged a narrow, windy path so we could blaze a larger, straighter path for others to follow. Our wish for the future of meetings is that the term "green meetings" won't be relevant anymore because it will simply be how meetings are produced. We hope you find this book an easy-to-follow map for your own journey to green meetings.

Learning Objectives

After reading this book, you should be able to:

a) understand the business case for green meetings and events;

b) know the choices/options that are available;

c) negotiate choices;

d) evaluate success;

e) improve cost-effectiveness;

f) create a vision for green meetings and events;

g) apply environmental principles to meeting and event planning; and

h) identify who benefits by implementing green meetings.

Overview

You've probably picked up this book because you've heard about green meetings and are curious, or your organization has taken on environmental policies and is looking toward green meetings, or you are personally passionate about the role you can play in taking better care of the Earth. In speaking to meeting and event professional groups around the world, we find it is usually the third reason – a personal passion or commitment – that gets you hooked. You've taken the first step to becoming a change agent!

The hospitality industry has a tremendous sphere of influence because meetings and events touch so many other industries. Think about how many industries we rely on to produce events:

- Energy — natural gas, electricity and oil used to produce meetings/hold events
- Transportation — airplanes, airports, cabs, buses, trains, rental cars
- Food — farms, dairy, cattle, poultry, fisheries
- Local community — employment, financial, retail
- Accommodations — hotels, cleaning products, the soft-goods market

The rates of consumption at meetings can be staggering. For instance, during a typical five-day conference, 2,500 attendees will use 62,500 plates, 87,500 napkins, 75,000 cups or glasses and 90,000 cans or bottles.[1] This little bit of trivia was a lesson learned by Nancy a few years back when bringing a conference to a convention center that served only disposable serviceware for groups of this size. The disposable products available were Styrofoam and #6 black plastic. She was calculating the number of alternative products when she was struck by the huge impact this one conference would have. Just one conference, in one city, for one week… WOW! What an opportunity each of us has to make a big impact.

We weren't alone in this realization. Large corporations are already beginning to understand and adopt new green initiatives as part of their long-range planning. General Electric's chair and CEO, Jeffrey Immelt, was quoted in May 2005 as saying, "It is no longer a zero-sum game – things that are good for the environment are also good for business. General Electric is embarking on this initiative not because it is trendy or moral, but because it will accelerate economic growth." [2]

GE is a great illustration because it is not necessarily considered an environmentally minded organization and Immelt admits he is no environmentalist. Organizations including The Home Depot, Starbucks, Interface Carpets, VNU Expo, Stetson Convention Services and many others now have sustainability departments, green teams or some other unit devoted to reducing their environmental impact. If you think greening is a perspective that only environmentalists and fringe groups have, think again.

FAST FACT

 BRUSSELS, Feb. 20, 2007 - Business leaders across Europe think that protecting the environment should be the number-one priority for global political leaders, according to the results of the 16th annual UPS Europe Business Monitor.

When asked which issues should be the highest on global political leaders' list of priorities, 45 percent of Europe's top business executives agreed on environmental protection, followed by 40 percent mentioning sustaining economic growth.[3]

So what does this have to do with meetings and events? Everything! Green meetings and events hold a hope for the future by reducing their impact on the environment and improving financial outcomes for our organizations. By adopting just one environmentally responsible practice, you can reduce both the consumption of the Earth's resources and your organization's expenses – a win-win situation for everyone. This chapter will explore how you can shape your organization's meetings to be more sensitive to the environment and play a positive role in the communities in which your meetings are held.

What are Green Meetings and Events?

When most people think of being "green" or environmentally sensitive, recycling is usually the first thing that comes to mind. A green meeting or event goes beyond recycling.

"Greening" a meeting or event encompasses all aspects of the strategic planning process. By making choices at every level of planning, from site selection to serving condiments like ketchup, mustard and sugar from bulk containers, you can significantly reduce the environmental impact of the event. Green meetings also incorporate social aspects including charitable

2

contribution and humanitarian efforts. There are many ways that meetings can have a positive impact in the communities where they are held. Well-planned volunteer activities can incorporate fun and instill a sense of common purpose and goodwill within a group while supporting a worthy cause. For the purposes of this chapter, both environmentally and socially responsible meetings and events are included in the term "green meetings."

Dispelling the Myths

While many organizations are working to make their meetings and events more eco-efficient, misconceptions about environmental practices are barriers for many others. During our work with clients over the past seven years, we have found these myths fall into five categories. While working to green your meetings, you may encounter one or all of the "myths of green meetings":

- **Myth 1: Environmentally responsible meetings are too expensive.**
  Many green strategies actually reduce rather than increase expenses. The simple act of asking a hotel to change sheets and towels by request rather than on a daily basis reduces the environmental impact, saves the hotel money and empowers the attendee – all at no cost to the host organization.

- **Myth 2: If conservation cannot be 100 percent, why bother?**
  In fact, every effort toward sustainability has an impact. According to Green Suites International, if one hotel adopts the bath and linen program mentioned above, 200 barrels of oil are saved per year – enough to run a family car for 180,000 miles (289,682 kilometers).

- **Myth 3: Eco-efficiency requires too much effort.**
  Most green practices are a matter of setting environmentally oriented policies and letting hotels and vendors know they are an important selection criterion. Green practices can become a part of the normal meeting management cycle, from site inspections and contract negotiations to promotion and logistical management.

- **Myth 4: Only "environmental types" are making efforts to go green.**
  Not true. For example, Fortune 500 hotel chains are participating in environmental benchmark programs through The Prince of Wales International Business Leaders Forum. Sustainability is keeping company with mega-retailers such as The Home Depot, which is committed to selling only wood from sustainable forests.

- **Myth 5: Individuals are powerless to change their workplaces and communities.**
  The burgeoning green marketplace is filled with success stories of individuals who came up with environmental solutions and helped meet the growing need for earth-friendly products and services. Empowerment is a primary goal of eco-efficient event management, giving attendees the opportunity to reduce their own environmental impact and adopt responsible behaviors. These individual changes continue beyond a single event.

Benefits of Green Events

Whether you are a planner or a supplier, producing green meetings can be rewarding by providing economic and environmental savings and increasing your organization's competitive advantage. However, green meetings must make business sense in order to be sustained.

Economic Benefits

For a planner, green meeting practices offer a variety of cost-saving opportunities without compromising quality. For example, selecting lodging properties within walking distance to events can eliminate thousands of dollars in shuttle services. The added benefit is attendees get a chance to get some fresh air and a little exercise, and see more of the surrounding area. There are many other cost-saving green practices you might want to consider. For example, eliminating individual bottled water service not only saves money but also is environmentally friendly. Instead, provide a refillable individual container (a great sponsorship opportunity) with large containers of water. This practice can save hundreds or thousands of dollars/euros depending on the size of the group. Another practice is to eliminate or significantly reduce speaker handouts. Make handouts available on a USB key or online during or after the event, saving both time and money. These two ideas represent a sampling of possible economic savings from green meetings. The intention is to get you thinking about potential opportunities to reduce stress on the environment without reducing service to your attendees.

Suppliers, especially hoteliers, have a multitude of green money-saving opportunities available to them. For hotels adopting environmentally responsible practices, energy efficiency, water conversation and waste management offer the most cost savings. Green Seal (www.greenseal.org) is a great resource for information about the savings associated with such practices for hotels. To help organizations estimate savings potential, Green Seal, which also offers green hotel certification, has developed averages for a 296-room hotel:

Water savings: Replacing 3.5-gallon-per-flush (gpf) toilets with 1.6 gpf toilets results in 307,914 gallons (1,165,581 liters) of water saved per year, or a cost savings of US$1,200 (€885) annually.

Energy savings: Replacing lobby lights with compact fluorescent bulbs saves US$735 (€541) annually plus the cost of maintenance staff time, and results in a drop in heat generated in the lobby.[5]

However, you do not need to be a hotelier to realize economic savings by incorporating green meeting practices. Caterers, food service providers and general service contractors have ample opportunities as well. For example, condiments served in bulk containers instead of individual containers can offer up to 50% savings. By providing online exhibitor kits, general services contractors save money in production time, mailing and staff time by not having to produce hard-copy versions.

These represent a very small sample of the economic savings realized from implementing green meeting practices. Suppliers should examine how and what they provide to their clients and customers, and then look for ways to go green. Consider alternatives that provide the same or greater level of service while minimizing the negative affects on the environment.

FAST FACT

Planners benefit by decreasing costs when planning a green meeting. Here's an example of a conference that used strategies that saved money and minimized environmental impacts. The Green Meeting Industry Council measured its savings for the 2007 Greening the Hospitality Conference with more than 100 attendees. The economic savings alone totaled US$6,410 (€4.717),[6] as you can see below:

Item	Green Practice	Savings
Lanyards	Reused lanyards; will not have to buy any for next year's conference	US$140 (€103)
Signs	Signs were printed without a date and have been reused for two years	US$340 (€251)
Registration	Online registration and promotion, saving the cost of mailings and postage	US$2,830 (€2.080)
Conference Bags	None were used	US$1,240 (€913)
Water Bottles	Water was served in pitchers, saving the cost of bottled water	US$1,860 (€1.370)

Environmental Benefits

While some green meeting practices produce concrete, measurable financial savings, others are more subtle. For example, Amy found that by requesting that water glasses at a served meal not be pre-filled, a facility can save hundreds of gallons of drinking water for an event serving 2,200 attendees. The added benefit to this is that when the servers pour water for the guests, the guests perceive a higher level of service. Using china service instead of disposables with the same size group can eliminate more than 1,800 pounds (816 kilograms) of plastic products being sent to a landfill. If food composting is available for the same size group over a three-day period, as much as 6.5 tons (5.9 metric tons) of food waste could be diverted from a landfill.[7]

All of this is to illustrate the environmental impact you have in the decisions you make about products and services used at your events. Recognizing and relaying information about the economic and environmental savings realized at meetings can be a powerful message that can influence behavior and attitudes about how meetings are implemented.

Competitive Advantage

Producing green meetings can have a dual competitive advantage. Both planners and suppliers are beginning to realize the benefits of green event practices. From the planner perspective, organizing green events provides a personal advantage as it shows an elevated level of expertise. Organizations are discovering increased attendee satisfaction when implementing green event practices. In addition, organizations have realized that green events make for good public relations and press.

Planning green meetings can increase your value to your organization by demonstrating a state-of-the-art skill. Currently this skill is highly sought and puts you far ahead of the competition. Recording the economic and environmental savings as a result of green meeting practices additionally quantifies your ability as an innovative and successful planner.

Suppliers who have adopted green practices are realizing the dual benefits of green: less operating costs and increased marketability. Venues are now tracking both the savings and increased sales.

FAST FACT

The Doubletree Hotel & Executive Meeting Center Portland – Lloyd Center has successfully taken on green initiatives – both saving them money and bringing in more business.

During the first six months of 2006, they redirected more than 126 tons of waste from the landfill, and saved almost $10,000 (€7.200). Hotel engineers have invested more than $245,000 (€176.661) in initiatives that have reduced energy use by 32 percent and saved $360,000 (€260.584). By installing low-flow showerheads in all 476 rooms and replacing 200 toilets with water-conserving 1.6-gallons-per-flush (6.0-liters-per-flush) toilets, staff has reduced total water usage by 15 percent.

According to Doug Brecht, Director of Marketing, "We realized that there was a great market of customers demanding sustainability. I can track $500,000 (€360.540) in convention business we've earned in just the six months since we got our Green Seal certification!"[8]

Organizations can gain a competitive advantage by implementing an innovative, environmentally responsible event. Demonstrating a commitment to minimize the event's ecological footprint gets people excited. Evaluations after green conferences for non-environmental groups have shown a marked increase in satisfaction levels, and many attendee comments specifically thanked organizers for taking environmentally responsible steps.[9] As one attendee put it, "Thanks, I recycle at home, don't change my sheets every day and don't use a new bar of soap each time I come home. I appreciate being able to continue the same practices while on the road."

Potential Regulation

The potential for regulation is very real. It is important to be ready before regulation becomes reality. Regulations have already been implemented in many parts of the world that affect energy usage and carbon emissions. Individual industries are also being impacted by regulations concerning natural resources and environmental practices.

The United Kingdom is working toward a British Standard Initiative (BSI) to accompany the ISO 14001 that relates to green meetings. ISO 14001 certification is an environmental management standard. Companies looking to achieve ISO14001 certification must identify elements of the business that impact on the environment and gain access to the relevant environmental legislation, as well as produce objectives for improvement and a management program to achieve them, including regular reviews for continual improvement.

In the United States, federal agencies in several states have begun setting standards for government meetings to be held at green hotels and facilities. These requirements include minimum guidelines for planners. Even without local, national or international regulations, conference planners are now setting their own minimum green guidelines and including them in their request for proposal (RFP) or tender process.

FAST FACT

The U.S. EPA (Environmental Protection Agency) recently issued a mandate to its planners to consider how environmentally friendly a venue is when buying meeting and conference services. With an agency budget of $51 million for travel, this mandate is certain to have a positive financial impact on meeting spending.[10]

Test Your Knowledge

1. What is a green meeting?
2. What is the business case for green meetings?
3. Who benefits by implementing green meetings?

2

Getting Started

OK, getting started can be the scariest part — we hear that over and over again. But it's not scary at all, if you remember this: It's just another aspect of planning a meeting or event. A "filter," if you will. Look at it this way: You're going to choose a venue, order food and beverage, and invite attendees. You may also choose an exhibit decorator, transportation company and hotel accommodations. These may require a request for proposal, site inspection and most likely a contract. You do all those things daily. Now do the exact same things through the green "filter." Add a few questions to the RFP about the venue's environmental policies; ask the caterer for a sustainable menu; invite attendees electronically instead of on a printed document. There's no need to reinvent the wheel — just make sure it treads lightly.

As with any conference or event, setting goals and objectives is essential to producing a successful event. During this process, make sure green meeting practices are incorporated as well. If the sponsoring organization is greening the meeting for the first time, they can begin by establishing the commitment of the organization to go green. Once the organization's level of support is received, you have full license to determine what green strategies or practices to put into place.

Start by understanding how greening your events will fit into your company's or your client's mission and values. Chances are that some environmental commitment, however subtle, may already exist. For example, Intel's mission states, "We strive to conserve natural resources and reduce the environmental burden of waste generation and emissions to the air, water and land." Alternately, 3M expresses, "It is 3M policy to provide a safe and healthful workplace for all, and to minimize the impact of our production processes and products on the environment." Use these mission statements and those of your sponsors to enroll stakeholders.

Chart the Course

Here are some fundamental questions to ask when leading your organization's stakeholders through the goals and objectives for green meetings:

- **Why does the organization want to incorporate green practices?**
  This question may seem self-explanatory, but ask it anyway. The answers received may be different than expected, and will shape the approach you take. For example, is the reason member- or attendee-driven? Is the board or CEO asking for it to be green? Are there external influences impacting the organization's image?

- **How much is the organization willing to contribute?**
  Is the organization willing to commit financially, if necessary, to support green event practices? Though many green practices produce cost savings, the decision to serve organic food, for example, may cost more. In some cities, asking for china service versus disposables costs more (don't get us started on this crazy rule). It is extremely helpful to know if the organization is willing to spend more resources if some of the green practices recommended cost more than traditional practices.

  Although it may be difficult to provide potential cost increases upfront, knowing approximately what the organization is willing to spend will save a lot of time and effort and focus the planning on appropriate practices. It will be easy to show a budget of cost savings versus expenditures for green practices.

- **Is this a one-time effort, or part of the organization's core practices?**
  This question clarifies the company's long-term commitment and purpose for adopting greening practices. You can build on any level of commitment. If the intention is to green all future events, the learning curve for the first one should make it easier next time.

  If this is a one-time effort you should caution the organization that greening an event is most successful if you build on the successes of each event. For example, if attendees know you are greening the current year's event and the event is not greened in subsequent years, it can become an uncomfortable situation. The expectation has been established and attendees may be enthusiastic about future efforts.

- **What components of the event do they see as the most important to green?**
  The answer to this question will provide direction and focus on where to spend time and resources. Showing success in an area that is considered important — for whatever reason — may lead to greater support in the future.

  For example, is it to have recycling in the meeting venue? Is it to offer organic, local food and china service? Is it reducing paper by not sending out a four-color, multi-page brochure? Or perhaps providing a carbon offset program for attendees' travel?

These questions will get you started. As green meeting strategies are incorporated in subsequent events and your knowledge increases, be open to exploring other questions. You're the event professional; stakeholders will look to you for both ideas and direction. What a wonderful place to be!

Once your organization has established the level of commitment to green the events, work to build on this by developing a green strategy for the organization's events. It's easier to get financial and management support if you develop a greening plan, as it will show how you will deploy environmental practices. Sometimes the best way to enroll and engage the organization is to start with one or two new practices, with the intention of building on their success.

Use the business case: the economic, environmental, competitive advantage and potential for regulation to influence organizations, clients or sponsors. Explain how implementing green events can cause them and/or their organization to be viewed as leaders. (For more information on the business case, read Chapter 1.)

FAST FACT

In 2002, the U.S. Green Building Council decided to take on green for their annual convention for the first time. That year they started with the basics: towel and linen reuse programs at hotels, china service for meals, eco-friendly cleaning products, a carbon offset program and recycled-content name badges. With each subsequent year, they built upon their successes, adding more pronounced and comprehensive measures. Here is a brief summary highlighting new practices they added:

2003: *Attendee lists and speaker bios posted online instead of printed; presentations distributed on CDs; bags made of recycled materials; biodegradable trash liners; recycled-content carpet.*

2004: *Shuttles fueled with biodiesel; food composting; biodegradable shipping and handling materials offered to exhibitors.*

2005: *Instituted permanent recycling programs at convention center and two hotels; caterer permanently switched to biodegradable serviceware; exhibitor binders made of post-consumer recycled fiber.*

2006: *Created a green exhibitor award; offered ride-sharing program to attendees; off-site events powered by fuel cells.[7]*

Set the Standards

The next step is to develop minimum guidelines to incorporate in all events. You should create criteria for all the vendors used, including convention centers, hotels, caterers, transportation services and even convention and visitors bureaus. The Convention Industry Council's Green Meetings Report offers helpful guidelines in eight areas of planning.[4] It's important that your guidelines are part of any initial conversations with destinations, convention and visitors bureaus, vendors, etc. Remember to include the guidelines in the RFP/Tender stage of planning. This will make negotiating and implementing the practices much easier.

Establishing minimum guidelines for green events will also help you measure the progress of greening events. Use the guidelines as a deciding factor in selecting vendors. Be sure to let suppliers who were not selected know why they were not selected.

Create minimum guidelines in all eight key categories below (based on the Convention Industry Council's Green Meeting Report guidelines).

- Destination Selection
- Accommodations Selection
- Meeting and Venue Selection
- Transportation Selection
- Food and Beverage Selection
- Exhibition Production
- Communications and Marketing
- On-site Office Procedures

We will go through each of these categories in subsequent chapters. Begin by choosing just one practice per category, if that feels more comfortable. Or choose several practices for one and fewer for another; it's up to you. We always begin by choosing what we call the "low-hanging fruit," choosing the easiest and most rewarding first.

As an example, take Accommodations Selection. Your minimum guidelines for your conference can be to always choose a hotel with a towel and sheet reuse program. Include this on your RFP.

By choosing a hotel that offers this service, you're saving both environmentally and economically (although the hotel may not pass along its savings in labor, energy or water use). Or your minimum guideline might be to choose a hotel within walking distance of the meeting venue and accessible via public transportation to/from the airport, saving both the environment and money by not hiring shuttle buses or paying for rental cars or taxi cabs.

Now let's look at Communications and Marketing. Your minimum guidelines might be to use an online registration system so that the process is paperless. You may already be doing this, because technology is moving that direction. Take a look at another minimum guideline, such as printing any necessary conference materials on 100% post-consumer paper. There are some great calculators online to see how many trees you can save just by switching to a new paper stock.

You get the idea. Some of the conferences we manage have extensive minimum guidelines, and some have fewer than 10. Start small and build upon your success. No event is 100 percent green, but each small step makes a significant difference.

Communicate Objectives

You'll need to communicate expectations for the event very clearly, especially if greening practices are new. Communicate with your own organization first. Let them know what policies or new practices are being put into place to green the event, why they are important, and the plan to implement them. Clear communication can establish expectations for your event and help to enroll stakeholders in the process.

Be sure to say the same thing to all the parties involved. The better they understand the goals and reasons, the more motivated they will be to implement these requests. After all, everyone wants the event to be successful.

This also happens with properties that have adopted greening practices. Nancy was on a site inspection for a conference that had high green expectations. This was one of the reasons the venue even made it to the site inspection phase. During the site inspection, Nancy began to ask about environmental practices at the facility. The salesperson was completely unaware of any green practices, including recycling, towel and sheet reuse, and energy savings measures. Even after being shown the RFP response, the salesperson still didn't have any firsthand knowledge of the policies. The property lost a large piece of business to a competitor property that easily talked about their green commitment. The general manager of the first property called to apologize for the salesperson not knowing, but it should be been communicated to all staff as the way the property did business.

Make sure to inform attendees. Attendees will be more engaged in the greening efforts if the what, why and how are communicated to them. Let them know why the organization is doing things differently, and why it is important to make a change. Attendees do not usually respond well to surprises, but they frequently are open to new practices and ideas if they are explained well. Attendees will be engaged and enrolled if they understand why the event may be different than in the past.

Informing the media about greening efforts could offer a press-worthy angle to the meeting. Consider writing a case study outlining the purpose of the meeting, what decisions were made to green the meeting, who participated in the greening efforts, what was accomplished, what lessons were learned and what measured results will be achieved. Case studies can be used as an after-meeting selling tool on the organization's Web site or as a press release. The press – and, in fact, the entire meetings industry – is anxious for measurable results from greening. Tell them!

Negotiate Green Practices

As we discussed earlier, each phase of meeting and event planning incorporates green components. The next step – the negotiation phase – is not different. But remember that many of your organization's greening practices may be new to your suppliers. Know what practices your organization is willing to compromise on and which ones they are not willing to relinquish. Also, be aware of which practices are easily implemented and are cost-saving or cost-neutral.

For example, there may be resistance or refusal from the food and beverage provider to donate food because of a perceived liability issue. In the United States there is a national Good Samaritan Law that was written to support the donation of food in good faith. The law provides liability protection for organizations that donate food to charity. Please note that there are areas in the world where food donation is not legal, so it varies from country to country; be sure to check the facts where you are. If food donation is against a vendor's policy even when it's legal to donate, the planner may decide that vendor is not a good fit.

As mentioned previously, most green practices are actually cost-saving or cost-neutral for suppliers. Use the cost savings as leverage in negotiations. For example, serving items in bulk instead of individual packets can save 50 percent or more. In many parts of the United States, recycling is less expensive for a facility than sending garbage to a landfill.

FAST FACT

The crucial component to remember when negotiating green efforts is to ensure they are included in your contracts. Make sure to include an environmental clause in the contract, with measurable results and consequences for non-performance. Alternatively, offer an incentive for complying with the agreed-upon green practices.

The sample contract language included here is for guidance on what to include in an environmental clause or addendum of a contract. You will need to modify the language to fit the laws of your country. All contract language should be reviewed and approved by legal counsel.

SHOW MANAGEMENT is committed to conducting an environmentally responsible meeting. DECORATOR agrees to support that goal through environmentally responsible procedures and practices of its services and its employees, vendors and contractors. DECORATOR agrees to work collaboratively with SHOW MANAGEMENT for the duration of this contract to improve the overall environmental performance and efficiency of the DECORATOR'S services. DECORATOR agrees to support the commitment internally by engaging and educating all departments of the Decorator DECORATOR'S services about this special commitment.

DECORATOR will implement the following procedures and practices during the conference.
- *Minimize Energy Use* – Lights, power and HVAC will be reduced during move-in and move-out times in the exhibit hall.

- *Exhibitor Kits/Service* – Kits will be available electronically via the Web site. Any binders that are mailed to exhibitors will be made from

35 percent post-consumer recovered fiber and recycled paper. The contents of the binder will be printed on post-consumer recycled paper, using vegetable-based inks.

- *Tabletop Coverings* – Coverings will be tabletop vinyl pre-cut to length, and wooden tables and biodegradable trash can liners will be used.

Track Efforts, Measure Results

The last step is measuring the results – don't skip this step. Tracking both the environmental and economic impacts provides the ability to quantify the results. Just as you provide a post-conference report and budget reconciliation, measuring greening results is important. For example, track the pounds of waste recycled or how much money was saved by eliminating conference bags. Ask attendees for feedback. Did the attendees notice and like any of the changes? Do they have suggestions for next time?

Once on site for the meeting, tour the back-of-the-house again to see how green practices will be implemented. Be sure to ask for measured data, such as how much cardboard, paper, plastic and aluminum are collected from the event. If your group is not the only one in the house, actual numbers may be difficult to obtain; in that case, ask for estimates. Ensure the organic and local food that is ordered is purchased and used, and that all environmental guidelines established are followed.

Then publish what was measured. People love data. Tell attendees, use the information on the sponsoring organization's Web site or as marketing for next time, share it with the team or organization, and tell their suppliers. Sharing the measured results is a great way to enroll and engage the sponsoring organization to want more greening action. This multilevel approach moves the notion of "greening" a meeting from a fringe behavior or perspective to a mainstream practice.

FAST FACT – Saving Plastic, Saving Money

By offering pitchers of water instead of bottled water, a 1,100-person conference over three days can save more than 8,000 bottles and more than $40,000![12]

One tool which we use to measure results from an event is the MeetGreen[SM] Calculator. It breaks down environmental practices for conferences into eight categories. The calculator provides a quantitative look at how many of those practices were requested, implemented and the measured outcomes. Below is an example of a report from one of our client events summarizing the scores for each of the categories. Whether you use this tool or another way of measuring your environmental impact, the more you communicate your results the better.

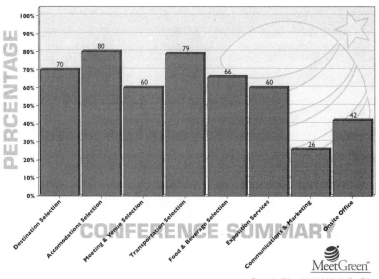

Conference Summary Report

Reproduction of this report must include the MeetGreen℠ logo
Copyright 2006 Meeting Strategies Worldwide Inc.

Utilize Resources

There is no need to re-invent the wheel when adopting green practices. Many resources are now available that provide sources for products and services, information about best practices, and opportunities to network with other industry professionals. When starting research on a new city, ask the convention and visitors bureau for a list of environmentally responsible vendors, including meeting venues and hotels. Utilize some of the same resources you would use for traditional meeting planning.

A comprehensive list of resources is included in the appendix of this book.

Start Now!

As we have talked about, the key to getting started is to just start. Think of green meeting practices not as another thing to add to a to-do list. Rather, incorporate the practices into the planning processes you already use. Even if you're only able to implement one environmentally responsible practice, you will have made a difference.

We applaud you for taking the first step on this journey! Our goal throughout the remainder of this book is to walk you through each of the event planning categories and further outline potential green practices and how to incorporate them.

Test Your Knowledge

1. What are the steps to getting started in incorporating and implementing green meeting practices?
2. How will you sell or convince clients to green their meetings?
3. What steps will you take to convince suppliers to support the green meeting practices?

3

Destination Selection

Does the location of the meeting really make a difference? Absolutely it does. Choosing a destination that is conducive to the event's purpose, is an environmentally responsible destination, and takes into account the location of attendees is integral to producing a green meeting.

Consider the Issues

The following are important factors in the decision-making process for site or destination selection.

- **Understand the event's purpose and the attendees' geographic locations.**
  When choosing a destination ensure it meets the organization's purpose for the meeting. Is it a board retreat, a fundraiser, an incentive trip, a live event, or an industry conference? The answer to this question will let you know where in the world to hold the event and how close to mass transit or an airport is appropriate.

  What are the demographics of the attendees? Determine a site that requires minimal travel for all participants.

- **Obtain a list of environmentally responsible organizations.**
  Ask the convention and visitors bureau or a destination management company (DMC) for a list of venues, properties and suppliers that have environmental practices in place. More and more destinations are developing a list of green organizations. If the list is not available, your request is an excellent opportunity to drive the demand for green meetings and will provide an indication of how environmentally responsible the location is.

- **Include environmental criteria in the RFP and contracts.**
  When sending out the RFP for events, you should include the environmental criteria. Specify the importance of environmental criteria in the site-selection process. For example, ask if recycling is available and implemented in the venues that are being considered. (Details of specific environmental criteria are discussed in each of the remaining categories.)

Cities that understand the importance of eco-friendly meetings will be more effective partners as you move into other aspects of managing the event. For accountability, it is important that green practices are included in contract language with all vendors.

- **Evaluate all aspects of the city and venue.**
  Weigh all the factors related to the city. Is the city's mass transit system adequate? Is it linked to the airport? Does the city publish walking maps? Are hotels and restaurants within walking distance of the venue or accessible via public transportation?

While it is unrealistic to believe that all destination decisions will be made based on environmental considerations alone, these factors can be important when choosing between comparable cities. The more a city and venue understand and embrace environmentally responsible practices, the easier it will be to green the event. If you eventually choose a city or venue based on environmental considerations, communicate this fact. It is important for cities and venues to know they either gained or lost business because of their commitment to the environment.

It is much more difficult to green a meeting once the destination is chosen and contracts are signed. As an example, we were hired to help implement green practices for a large faith-based organization with its annual members assembly for 6,000 delegates. The city, venues and hotels had been chosen several years before – not uncommon. Amy quickly realized there was no recycling available in the city, making recycling efforts more difficult. Amy was able, however, to find a local waste hauler interested in starting a recycling business. She was also able to convince the convention center to let the hauler remove the recycling without any additional fees. The assembly was able to institute recycling for their conference. But it took hours of work and the cooperation of many to pull it off.

To ensure this type of effort will not be required in the future, the organization now includes recycling in the destination city as a minimum guideline in all requests for proposal.

The following page is a sample for designing a request for proposal (RFP) or tender requesting green meeting practices. Remember to incorporate the following green meeting practices into all meeting pre-planning tasks such as request for proposals, tenders, site inspections and contract negotiations.

Test Your Knowledge

1. List at least three factors to consider in evaluating the environmental aspects of a destination.

2. How would you find information about green suppliers?

3. In making your decision, what value would you place on whether the destination has existing green practices or at least is willing to implement them for the meeting?

MeetGreen^{SM} Minimum Guidelines – Destination Selection

Conference: **Conference Dates:**
City for Consideration:

The intended result of requiring MeetGreen^{SM} Strategies is to support the mission and values of <ORGANIZATION NAME> by practicing sustainable, responsible meeting management strategies. <ORGANIZATION NAME> is taking the opportunity to strengthen green meeting management practices by driving the meeting and convention market to adopt environmentally responsible practices. The green strategies are customized for the <CONFERENCE NAME> and are categorized in the following five areas: air quality, energy efficiency, water conservation, waste minimization and environmental purchasing. These strategies focus primarily on site selection; a more complete set of guidelines will be presented further into the planning process.

Please note: MeetGreen^{SM} Strategies should be offered at no additional cost to the organization. Preference will be given to sites with a maximum number of policies/practices in place. These strategies serve as minimally expected practices. Additional detailed strategies may be required. Compliance language to ensure implementation will be included in the final contract.

Please complete the following survey questions, indicating the level of green practices. Circle the number or statement according to the following key:	
1	Currently available and/or implemented
2	Will commit to implementation in time for the start of conference/event.
3	Currently not available, and no future plans to implement

MeetGreen^{SM} Minimum Guidelines – Destination Selection

Convention Center			
Air Quality			
Can the convention center provide documentation about air quality control and systems for convention center and hotels?	1	2	3
Energy Efficiency			
Are convention center and hotel properties located within walking distance or easily accessible by public transportation?	Y	N	
Is an energy-saving strategy in place for the convention center by reducing lights, power and HVAC during move-in and move-out in the exhibit hall?	1	2	3
Does the convention center minimize energy use by turning off lights in meeting rooms when not in use?	1	2	3
Water Conservation			
Does the convention center (or caterer at the convention center) offer large containers of drinking water rather than individual bottles?	1	2	3
Does the convention center have low-flow toilets and other water-saving devices in restrooms?	1	2	3
Does the convention center sweep rather than spray parking lots, sidewalks and driveways?	1	2	3
Waste Minimization			
Does the convention center have a recycling program to recycle glass, aluminum, plastic, paper, grease and cardboard?	1	2	3
Does the convention center have a policy to reduce and reuse where possible and appropriate, and minimize paper usage?	1	2	3
Is the convention center staff trained to implement environmental policies?	1	2	3
Will the convention center work with the organization at no cost to implement a composting system, if available?	Y	N	
Environmental Purchases			
Does the convention center purchase environmentally responsible bathroom supplies (minimum 20 percent recycled products for hand towels and toilet paper)?	1	2	3
Does the convention center purchase environmentally responsible cleaning products for carpets, floors, kitchens and bathrooms (minimum 50 percent of products are environmentally responsible)?	1	2	3
Does the convention center request vendors to have environmentally responsible practices? And support those who do?	1	2	3

MeetGreen^{SM} Minimum Guidelines – Destination Selection

Hotels			
Air Quality			
Are the hotel/s located within walking distance of the convention center or easily accessible by public transportation?	Y	N	
Will the hotels provide documentation about air quality control and systems?	1	2	3
Energy Efficiency			
Do the hotels instruct staff to shut off HVAC/lights when guests are not in their rooms?	1	2	3
Water Conservation			
Are water-conservation practices such as low-flow showerheads and toilets available in hotels?	1	2	3
Do the hotels offer and implement a towel and linen reuse program?	1	2	3
Waste Minimization			
Do the hotels implement a recycling program to recycle glass, aluminum, plastic, paper, grease and cardboard?	1	2	3
Do the hotels have a policy in place to reduce and reuse where possible and appropriate, and minimize paper usage?	1	2	3
Do the hotels participate in a food donation program?	1	2	3
Are hotel staffs trained to implement environmental practices?	1	2	3
Do the hotels serve food and beverage items such as juice, iced tea, coffee and water in pitchers rather than as individual servings? Do they serve condiments in bulk?	1	2	3
Will the hotels work with the organization at no cost to implement a composting system, if available?	1	2	3
Do the hotels replace unused amenities only when empty or asked by guests?	1	2	3
Do hotel food outlets ban serving food or beverages in polystyrene (Styrofoam) containers in banquet or take-out service?	1	2	3
Environmental Purchases			
Do the hotels purchase locally grown and organic foods and products wherever possible and affordable (minimum 15% of meals)?	1	2	3
Do the hotels purchase condiments and beverages in bulk?	1	2	3
Do the hotels offer sustainable menus with comparable prices?	1	2	3
Do the hotels purchase environmentally responsible bathroom supplies (minimum 20 percent recycled products for hand towels and toilet paper)?	1	2	3

MeetGreen^{SM} Minimum Guidelines – Destination Selection

Do the hotels purchase environmentally responsible cleaning products for carpets, floors, kitchens and bathrooms (minimum 50 percent of products are environmentally responsible)?	1	2	3
Do the hotels have an established program with wholesalers to utilize reusable crates or cartons?	1	2	3
Do the hotels request vendors have environmental practices in place?	1	2	3

Caterer

Water Conservation

Does the convention center caterer implement water-saving strategies (for example, not pre-filling water glasses, not providing saucers under coffee cups, or offering large containers of drinking water rather than individual bottles)?	1	2	3
Does the convention center caterer reduce the use of ice in drinking water?	1	2	3

Waste Minimization

Does the convention center caterer implement a recycling program to recycle glass, aluminum, plastic, paper, grease and cardboard?	1	2	3
Does the convention center caterer have a policy in place to reduce and reuse where possible and appropriate, and minimize paper usage?	1	2	3
Does the convention center caterer donate leftover food?	1	2	3
Is the convention center catering staff trained to implement environmental policies?	1	2	3
Does the convention center caterer serve juice, iced tea, coffee and water in pitchers and serve condiments in bulk?	1	2	3
Does the convention center caterer use china service? If not possible, do they use biodegradable disposable serviceware?	1	2	3
Will the convention center caterer work with the organization at no cost to implement a composting system if available?	1	2	3

Environmental Purchases

Does the convention center caterer purchase locally grown and organic foods and products wherever possible and affordable (minimum 15% of meals)?	1	2	3
Does the convention center caterer purchase condiments and beverages in bulk?	1	2	3
Does the convention center caterer offer sustainable menus with comparable prices?	1	2	3

Accommodations Selection

4

Choosing environmentally responsible accommodations is the next important decision you will make. Guests often cite their experience with the hotel/ venue on evaluations; they consider it a reflection of your efforts to green the event. The venue's commitment to green practices provides tangible evidence of the environmental awareness of the sponsoring organization.

Additionally, green practices benefit accommodations locations not only by helping them present an environmentally responsible image to guests, but also by helping the location realize significant economic savings. In working with the accommodations personnel, it will be valuable to include the housekeeping, operations and food and beverage managers. They are often more knowledgeable about what is possible and feasible than the sales or convention service person. Most of the recommendations for properties are cost-saving or cost-neutral.

The location of the attendees' sleeping accommodations is often the same location where the meeting or event will take place. If the accommodations location is the same as the meeting venue, also consider the information in Chapter 5 – Meeting and Venue Selection, and Chapter 7 – Food and Beverage.

Make an Impact

The following are some basic environmentally responsible practices to include in the meeting's minimum guidelines. Most of these practices are cost-saving.

- **Linen and towel reuse program.** Guests are encouraged to decide whether their sheets and towels are changed daily or less frequently during their stay. By following the hotel's system, guests make their own choice. Always ask about the training program for housekeeping staff. It takes consistent training of housekeeping staff to make this program successful.

- **In-room energy savings program.** Also ask if the property has occupancy sensors in the guest rooms. If not, ensure hotel employees are instructed to shut the blinds, minimize heating/air conditioning, and turn off all lights while rooms are unoccupied.

- **Amenities.** Does the hotel have guestroom dispensers for soap, shampoo and lotion, or do they donate unused portions of amenities to charity? Request amenities to be replenished only as needed or requested. Some hotels in Europe actually refill guest amenity bottles.

- **Recycling program.** Does the venue routinely implement a recycling program for cardboard, paper, metal, glass and plastics? If not, is recycling available to them, and will they ensure it is implemented for the event?

- **In-room and property recycling programs.** Do they offer guests recycling in their room, including paper, metal, glass and plastic products? If in-room recycling is not available, the housekeeping or operations staff should sort these items after the room is cleaned. Guests should be told this is being done on their behalf. Determine if the hotel has a program to donate or reuse old linens, fixtures and furniture.

- **Paperless registration and communication.** Ask if the hotel has paperless check-in/-out and billing procedures. Also request to be e-mailed (rather than mailed) all banquet event orders (BEOs), contracts and master accounts. Finally, ask if in-room television service can be used to communicate to attendees.

General Guidelines

- **Environmental management program or certification.** Has the property been certified by a third-party organization, or have they established an environmental management program and training for all staff?

FAST FACT

Environmental certifications typically come in two varieties: facility and operations. Facility certification programs are based on the building itself. They take into consideration construction materials and waste as well as architectural elements designed to minimize the use of resources. Examples of this include using skylights to minimize electricity use and native plants that do not require extra watering to maintain. In the United States, the largest and most well recognized program is LEED certification by the U.S. Green Building Council. Operational certifications cover how environmentally responsible the day-to-day operations of a facility are. This can include things such as established green policies, recycling and donation programs, and use of compact fluorescent lighting.

However, not all green certifications and programs are created equal. They vary greatly in their requirements and stringency. Some programs require detailed applications and site inspections, while others will list a facility with no validation of practices. You should confirm the extent of oversight and documentation that a facility can provide to accompany their certification claim.

Examples of facility certification criteria

solar panels

abundant windows for natural lighting

reclaimed wood

native plants

Examples of operational certification criteria

CFLs

furniture made from sustainable wood

green cleaning supplies

recycle bins

composting

Many states and even national governments (outside the United States) now have green programs as well.

- **Environmentally responsible purchasing practices.** Ask the hotel if they have environmentally responsible purchasing practices. Generally speaking, environmentally responsible purchasing includes items that have minimal packaging (buying creamer in large containers and serving them it smaller containers); are non-toxic (earth-friendly cleaning supplies or low VOC paints); are made of recyclable materials (post-consumer recycled paper); are made of materials that can be recycled or composted (biodegradable food serviceware); or include energy-efficient equipment (compact fluorescent lighting).

FAST FACT

Compact fluorescent lamps (CFLs) use about 75 percent less energy than standard incandescent bulbs and produce 75 percent less heat. Hotels that use CFLs in sleeping rooms will rate better in accommodations selection.[13]

Conduct a site inspection to determine if practices and policies are in place. Experience has taught many planners to conduct a back-of-the-house tour as part of the green site inspection. It is important to actually see where the recycling is sorted and where it is stored before pick-up. Take a look at the kitchen to see the amount of individual packaging that is used, as well as the venue's recycling or composting efforts, and where they store food for donation to local food banks.

We cannot express the need for inspection enough. Once, after being reassured that recycling was happening and even seeing the bins in the front-of-house, we found the material from these bins being dumped straight into the trash.

Include environmental commitment as a factor in rating properties. Weigh each hotel or venue's environmental policies and procedures along with other determining factors. Ask hotels that do not already have policies in place if it is possible to establish them for the meeting. Ask if they will continue them after the requesting group checks out. The following pages include an example of minimum guidelines for a hotel and a more in-depth survey to ascertain the level of environmental practices the hotel has.

Support hotels that have environmental policies in place or are willing to implement your environmental requests.

FAST FACT

In addition to supporting hotels willing to comply with green practices, Unitarian Universalists Association also advised delegates of those hotels that were unwilling to participate, including the following information

for delegates on their Web site: "Please be advised that the following hotel was unwilling to work with us in our efforts to promote environmental sustainability and so is not one of our contracted hotels."

Important note: When green practices have been agreed to by the venue, the next step is to ensure the contract supports the commitment. Even if a hotel has environmental practices in place, outline and include them in the contract and require them to be in place and implemented for your event. Whatever contract language is ultimately used, ensure that the expectations for what green practices are to be implemented and measured are clearly defined and some level of consequence is included for failure to comply.

For example:
Any programs in place at the time of signing will be in place at the time of the event, and HOTEL agrees to cooperate with enhancing any such programs. Failure to adhere to the stated green policies is considered in breach of contract and may result in compensation concessions for ORGANIZATION.

The following specific documentation is due within 30 days after the event to receive any final payments due HOTEL:
- Recycling weights/amounts for:
  o   Paper, plastic, glass, aluminum/cans, cardboard

- Waste, by weight, for: landfill (non-recyclable materials), food
- Amount of donated food in weight – if food/beverage were contracted as part of the conference
- Paper content of bathroom products
- Specifications of any biodegradable products used

A more detailed example of hotel contract language is included at the end of this chapter.

Test Your Knowledge

1. What are two common green requests to make to a hotel?

2. Who from the hotel should be included from the beginning when requesting green practices?

3. What should you do to ensure the green practices that the hotel agreed to will be implemented?

MeetGreen^{SM} Minimum Guidelines – Hotel

The goal of the MeetGreen^{SM} Hotel Minimum Guidelines is to identify environmental practices of hotels. The survey assesses the potential success in "greening" a meeting or conference. Please review the questions and answer them thoroughly. You may need to consult with several of the property's departments to complete the survey.

Hotel Name:
Contact Name:
Telephone Number:
E-Mail Address:
Fax Number:

Please complete the following survey questions, indicating the level of green practices. Circle the number or statement according to the following key:	
1	Currently available and/or implemented
2	Will commit to implementation in time for the start of conference/event.
3	Currently not available, and no future plans to implement

Hotels			
Does the hotel have environmentally responsible practices in place? If so, please provide a list.	1	2	3
Air Quality			
Is the hotel located within walking distance to convention center, other city attractions or easily accessible by public transportation?	Y	N	
Will the hotel provide documentation about air quality control and systems?	1	2	3
Energy Efficiency			
Does the hotel instruct staff to shut off HVAC/lights when guest rooms are vacant?	1	2	3
Does the hotel instruct staff to shut blinds/curtains when guest rooms are vacant?	1	2	3
Do guests rooms have occupancy sensors?	1	2	3
Water Conservation			
Does the hotel have water-conservation practices such as low-flow showerheads and toilets in place?	1	2	3
Does the hotel offer and implement a towel and linen reuse program?	1	2	3
Waste Minimization			
Does the hotel implement a recycling program to recycle glass, aluminum, plastic, paper, grease and cardboard?	1	2	3

MeetGreen^{SM} Minimum Guidelines – Hotel

Does the hotel have a policy in place to reduce and reuse where possible and appropriate, and minimize paper usage?	1	2	3
Is the hotel staff trained to implement environmental practices?	1	2	3
Does the hotel replace unused amenities only when empty or requested by guests?	1	2	3
Does the hotel offer bulk dispensers in guest rooms?	1	2	3
Environmental Purchases			
Does the hotel purchase environmentally responsible bathroom supplies (minimum 20 percent recycled products for hand towels and toilet paper)?	1	2	3
Does the hotel purchase environmentally responsible cleaning products for carpets, floors, kitchens and bathrooms (minimum 50 percent of products are environmentally responsible)?	1	2	3
Does the hotel have an established program with wholesalers to utilize reusable crates or cartons?	1	2	3
Does the hotel request vendors have environmental practices in place?	1	2	3

Food and Beverage			
Water Conservation			
Does the caterer implement water-saving strategies (for example, not pre-filling water glasses, not providing saucers under coffee cups, or offering large containers of drinking water rather than individual bottles)?	1	2	3
Does the caterer reduce the use of ice in drinking water?	1	2	3
Waste Minimization			
Does the caterer have a policy in place to reduce and reuse where possible and appropriate, and minimize paper usage?	1	2	3
Does the caterer donate leftover food?	1	2	3
Is the catering staff trained to implement environmental policies?	1	2	3
Does the caterer serve juice, iced tea, coffee and water in pitchers and serve condiments in bulk?	1	2	3
Does the caterer use china service (or, if not possible, use biodegradable disposable serviceware)?	1	2	3
Will the caterer work with the organization at no cost to implement a composting system if available?	1	2	3
Environmental Purchases			
Does the caterer purchase locally grown and organic foods and products wherever possible and affordable (minimum 15 percent of meals)?	1	2	3
Does the caterer purchase condiments and beverages in bulk?	1	2	3
Does the caterer offer sustainable menus with comparable prices?	1	2	3

MeetGreen^{SM} Hotel Green Practices Survey

The goal of the MeetGreen^{SM} Hotel Green Practices Survey is to identify environmental practices of hotels. The survey assesses the potential success in "greening" a meeting or conference. Please review the questions and answer them thoroughly. You may need to consult with several of the property's departments to complete the survey.

Hotel Name:
Contact Name:
Telephone Number:
E-Mail Address:
Fax Number:

1. ***General Hotel Operations/Water Conservation*** – What policies (e.g., low-flow showerheads and sink aerators) ensure water conservation? How are these policies communicated to guests?

2. ***General Hotel Operations/Energy Efficient Lighting*** – What steps are taken to conserve energy/lighting? Does this apply to all departments in the hotel? What percentage of your property's lighting is fluorescent?

3. ***General Hotel Operations/Renovation and Remodeling Materials*** – What environmentally responsible materials have been or are being used in renovations and remodeling?

4. ***General Hotel Operations/Recycling*** – What items are recycled? How is the hotel's recycling program implemented? Does your property have a recycling program that is offered to guests and meeting rooms? Does your property recycle materials such as linens, phone books, oil or pallets? How do you ensure that recycling occurs?

MeetGreen^{SM} Hotel Green Practices Survey

5. General Hotel Operations/Meeting Rooms – What steps are taken to ensure energy (for instance, lights, air conditioning and heat) is efficiently used in meeting rooms, particularly when meeting rooms are used for portions of the day? Are recycling bins provided in meeting rooms? Can you provide meeting tables without tablecloths?

6. General Hotel Operations/Staff Training – Is environmental policy and procedure training provided to hotel staff? Which departments take part in this training? Are all levels of staff trained? Please describe.

7. General Hotel Operations/Community Projects – What community projects does the hotel sponsor?

8. General Hotel Operations/Environmental Certification and Awards – Has your property earned environmental certification or won any environmental awards? If so, please describe.

9. General Hotel Operations/Donated Meeting Products – What policy is there to donate leftover or discarded meeting materials (for instance, office supplies or product samples)? How is it implemented?

10. General Hotel Operations/Other – Please list any other environmental policies for general hotel operations that are not covered in the above questions.

11. Purchasing/Recycled and Recyclable Products – What is the hotel's policy on purchasing recycled or recyclable products? What recyclable or recycled products are purchased?

MeetGreen^{SM} Hotel Green Practices Survey

12. Purchasing/Reusable and Durable Products – What is the hotel's policy on purchasing reusable and durable products? What reusable and durable products are currently purchased? Does your property donate, sell or recycle old durables (e.g., furnishings)?

13. Purchasing/Beverages – Does your property purchase and serve beverages in returnable, refillable containers? If beverage containers have deposits, who pays for them?

14. Purchasing/Organic Products – Are organic products purchased? Can organic products be purchased on request? If so, do you charge additional fees?

15. Purchasing/Locally Grown and Produced Products – What percentage of locally grown or produced products are used? Please list examples.

16. Purchasing/Fresh Produce – Will your kitchen purchase fresh rather than packaged produce?

17. Purchasing/Cleaning Products – Are all cleaning products purchased for the hotel environmentally safe? If not, please list what is being used.

18. Purchasing/Other – Please list other environmentally focused purchasing practices not covered in the above questions.

19. Food and Beverage/Service – Are bulk containers used? (For instance, during a coffee service, do you serve creamer in a pitcher and sugar in a bowl?) Will your property serve food family-style (one large plate) without garnishes?

20. Food and Beverage/Vegetarian or Vegan Options – Does your menu include vegetarian or vegan selections?

21. Food and Beverage/Reusable Items – Will food and beverage services use reusable items such as cloth, glass and ceramic rather than disposable items such as polystyrene or plastic?

22. Food and Beverage/Other – Please list any other measures taken to provide environmentally friendly food and beverage service.

23. Guest Services/In-Room Products and Amenities – Do your guestrooms have soap and shampoo dispensers? Would your property consider replacing small plastic amenity bottles with soap and shampoo dispensers in rooms occupied by event participants? Are housekeepers instructed not to replace soap, shampoo and other products until they are depleted?

24. Guest Services/In-Room Products and Amenities – What environmentally responsible products or amenities are provided in the guest rooms? (For example, are there glasses and mugs in guest rooms, rather than disposable paper cups? How are you reducing dry cleaning and laundry paraphernalia?)

25. Guest Services/Amenity Recycling Program – Is there a program for recycling amenities? (For instance, are leftover amenities donated to local homeless or domestic violence shelters?)

26. Guest Services/Linen and Towel Reuse Program – Does your hotel have a program in which guests can choose whether or not to have bath towels or bed linens changed? How are guests informed of the program?

MeetGreen^{SM} Hotel Green Practices Survey

27. *Guest Services/Check-In Procedures* – What procedures (for example, paperless check-in) are in place?

28. *Guest Services/Check-Out Procedures* – What procedures (for instance, video check-out) are currently in place?

29. *Guest Services/Business Center* – What environmentally sensitive products or services does the hotel business center offer guests (e.g., post-consumer/recycled paper, double-sided printing, energy efficient equipment)?

30. *Guest Services/Other* – Please list any other environmental policies not covered in the above questions.

MeetGreen^{SM} Contract Language - Hotel

Sample language provided as a guide – not intended to be construed as legal advice or documentation.

The organization (ORGANIZATION) is committed to conducting an environmentally responsible conference. The hotel (HOTEL) agrees to support that goal through environmentally responsible procedures and practices of HOTEL and its employees, vendors and contractors. HOTEL agrees to work collaboratively with ORGANIZATION for the duration of this contract to ensure that the environmental performance goals are met.

HOTEL agrees to support the commitment internally by engaging and educating all departments of HOTEL regarding this commitment. HOTEL will communicate to ORGANIZATION no later than 90 days before conference begins any barriers experienced for the requested environmental practices that may prevent HOTEL from complying.

Environmental Expectations
ORGANIZATION expects HOTEL will adhere to the following green practices which include: waste management, recycling, energy use, use of renewable resources and conservation of non-renewable resources. HOTEL agrees to provide and/or implement the following at no additional charge to ORGANIZATION:

- Recycling Participation –
    - o Provide a recycling program (recycling paper, plastic, glass, aluminum cans, cardboard and grease) for entire hotel, including sleeping rooms and meeting space.
    - o Provide clearly marked recycling containers in common areas including lobby and HOTEL guest rooms unless HOTEL sorts and recycles independently.

- Energy Use –
    - o Instruct HOTEL housekeeping staff to shut blinds and turn down the heat/air conditioning and turn off lights during the day in rooms while attendees are gone.
    - o Implement a towel and sheet reuse program.

MeetGreen^{SM} Contract Language - Hotel

- Waste Minimization –

    o Instruct the HOTEL housekeeping staff to not replace
      consumable amenities daily unless they are gone. Use of
      soap and shampoo dispensers would be optimal. HOTEL will
      participate in an amenity donation program, if available locally.

    o Use glass or china (non-disposable) catering plates, cups and
      glasses.

    o NO polystyrene (#6 plastic) used under any circumstances.

    o Serve condiments in bulk containers, not individual servings,
      eliminating wasteful packaging. This includes sugar, creamer,
      butter, cream cheese, etc. (exception: serve sugar substitutes in
      individual servings).

    o Use cloth napkins whenever possible. Use coasters instead of
      cocktail napkins. If paper napkins are required, then they must be
      made of post-consumer recycled paper.

    o Donate all leftover food to a local food bank.

    o Donate all table scraps to a local farm or compost – if a
      program is available or arranged for by ORGANIZATION.

    o If food and beverage events are not booked in hotel, hotel is to
      offer locally grown, organic option in food and beverage outlets.
      Polystyrene is not to be used in any venue of the hotel.

- Environmentally Responsible Purchasing –

    o Use cleaning products that do not introduce toxins into the air
      or water.

    o Use shade-grown coffee at any conference functions.

    o Use predominately local, organic produce/products in any food
      and beverage events contracted as a part of the conference.

Any programs in place at the time of signing will be in place at the time of the
event, and HOTEL agrees to cooperate with enhancing any such programs.
Failure to adhere to the stated green policies is considered in breach of
contract and may result in compensation concessions for ORGANIZATION.

MeetGreen^{SM} Contract Language - Hotel

The following specific documentation is due within 30 days after the event to receive any final payments due HOTEL:

- Recycling weights/amounts for:
    - o   Paper, plastic, glass, aluminum/cans, cardboard

- Waste, by weight, for: landfill (non-recyclable materials), food
- Amount of donated food in weight – if food and beverage were contracted as part of the conference
- Food weight that was composted – if composting was available and if food and beverage were contracted as part of the meeting
- Number of ORGANIZATION'S guests participating in the towel/sheet reuse program
- Percentage of locally grown products used in food and beverage services – if food and beverage were contracted as part of the conference
- Percentage of organically grown products used in food/beverage services – if food and beverage were contracted as part of the conference
- Paper content of bathroom products
- Specifications of any biodegradable products used

Meeting & Venue Selection

The location of the meeting plays a significant role in the success of the event. Meeting venues can be small facilities, town halls, hotels, sports stadiums, conference or convention centers. For the purposes of this chapter, convention centers were selected as the example used. However, the information covered should be transferable to most venues. If the meeting venue is also the accommodation location, please see the previous chapter on accommodations.

Start the conversation about green during the first contact.
In the initial discussions with the venue remember to include green meeting expectations. Ensure minimum green guidelines are part of the request for proposal or tender asking the venue to respond to the guideline requests.

Weigh each venue's environmental policies and procedures along with other determining factors.
Ask venues that do not already have policies in place if it is possible to establish them for your meeting and ask if they will continue them after your group leaves.

Conduct a site inspection to determine if practices and policies are in place.
As already mentioned, experience has taught us to conduct a back-of-the-house tour as part of the site inspection. It is important to actually see how waste is managed and water and energy are conserved. Tour the kitchen to see the amount of individual packaging, recycling or composting efforts, and where they store food for donation to local food banks.

Additionally, let the venue know that although most green practices help present an environmentally responsible image to clients, more importantly, the venue should also experience economic savings. Many of the recommendations are cost saving or cost neutral. In working with the venue personnel it will be valuable to include the cleaning, operations and food and beverage managers in the planning stages to implementing green practices. They are often more knowledgeable about what is possible and feasible than the sales or convention service person.

Ensure practices are occurring and the measurable data is being tracked.
Once onsite for the meeting, tour the back-of-the-house again to see how green practices are implemented. Be sure to ask for measured data such as how much cardboard, paper, plastic and aluminum are collected and recycled from your event. If your group is not the only one in house, actual numbers may be more difficult, but ask for them to give you estimates.

This is an example of a sign that can be posted by recycling bins to indicate what items may be recycled.

Venue Practices

Some key questions to ask the venue are as follows:
- Environmental management program or certification. Has the property been certified by a third-party organization or have they established an environmental management program and training for all staff?

For more information regarding the different categories of environmental certifications, read the Fast Fact box in Chapter 4.

- **Recycling program.** Does the venue routinely implement a recycling program for cardboard, paper, metal, glass, and plastics? If not, is it available to them and will they ensure one is implemented for the event?

- **Energy conservation practices.** Does the venue have a policy to reduce HVAC useage while exhibits are moving in and out? Are occupancy sensors employed in meeting and sleeping rooms to turn off lighting and adjust temperatures when the room is vacant? Are compact fluorescent lights routinely used in all rooms?

- **Water conservation practices.** Other environmental factors to consider are water usage and the products and services purchased to produce the show. Food and beverage service and restroom usage are among the larger contributions to water usage during an exhibition. Planners should consider facilities and caterers that have water conservation practices in place. For food and beverage practices, see chapter 7. Examples of water conservation practices for a facility would include: low-flow toilets, sinks, sweeping not spraying driveways or parking lots.

- **Restroom service.** Ask the venue if they provide alternatives to paper hand towels such as hand dryers or linen hand towels. For their paper products, are the made with a recycled content? Does the venue use automated sinks and dispensers? Do they use environmentally friendly cleaning products?

- **Environmentally responsible purchasing practices.** Ask the venue about their environmentally responsible purchasing practices. General speaking, environmentally responsible purchasing includes items that have minimal packaging, are non toxic (earth-friendly cleaning supplies or low VOC paints), made of recyclable materials (post-consumer recycled toilet paper), are made of materials that can be recycled or energy efficient equipment (compact fluorescent light bulbs).

SUCCESS STORY

 Nearly 4,000 attendees and 148 exhibiting companies from across the nation participated in the inaugural Sierra Summit 2005 produced by the Sierra Club. The four-day meeting was held in the Club's birth place, San Francisco, CA.

An estimated 80% of waste was diverted and only 2,780 pounds of garbage went to the landfill. The efforts and ability to compost all disposable items increased the average recycling numbers by 5% at the convention facility. This is a legacy that the Summit should be proud of building.[16]

Specify environmental programs in the contract.
Once green practices have been agreed to by the venue, the next step is to ensure the contract supports the commitment. Include a clause in the contract outlining the environmental programs to be in place during your event; be clear about the impact of non-compliance. Be sure whatever contract language is ultimately used that the expectations about what green practices are to be implemented and measured are clearly defined.

Test Your Knowledge

1. When do you discuss your green meeting expectations with the venue?

2. What is the next step once the venue has agreed to implement green practices?

3. What should you do to verify the green practices are being implemented?

MeetGreen^{SM} Minimum Guidelines – Convention Center

Conference: **Conference Dates:**
City for Consideration:

The intended result of requiring MeetGreen^{SM} Strategies is to support the mission and values of <ORGANIZATION NAME> by practicing sustainable, responsible meeting management strategies. <ORGANIZATION NAME> is taking the opportunity to strengthen green meeting management practices by driving the meeting and convention market to adopt environmentally responsible practices. The green strategies are customized for the <CONFERENCE NAME> and are categorized in the following five areas: air quality, energy efficiency, water conservation, waste minimization and environmental purchasing. These strategies focus primarily on site selection; a more complete set of guidelines will be presented further into the planning process.

Please note: MeetGreen^{SM} Strategies should be offered at no additional cost to the organization. Preference will be given to sites with a maximum number of policies/practices in place. These strategies serve as minimally expected practices. Additional detailed strategies may be required. Compliance language to ensure implementation will be included in the final contract.

Please complete the following survey questions, indicating the level of green practices. *Circle the number or statement according to the following key:*	
I	Currently available and/or implemented
2	Will commit to implementation in time for the start of conference/event.
3	Currently not available, and no future plans to implement

Convention Center			
Air Quality			
Has the ability to provide documentation about air quality control and systems for convention center and hotels	I	2	3
Energy Efficiency			
Are convention center and hotel properties located within walking distance of each other or easily accessible by public transportation?	Y	N	
Is an energy-saving strategy in place for the convention center by reducing lights, power and HVAC during move-in and move-out in the exhibit hall?	I	2	3
Does the convention center minimize the energy use by turning off lights in meeting rooms when not in use?	I	2	3

45

MeetGreen^{SM} Minimum Guidelines – Convention Center

Water Conservation			
Does the convention center (or caterer at the convention center) offer large containers of drinking water rather than individual bottles?	1	2	3
Does the convention center have low-flow toilets and other water-saving devices in restrooms?	1	2	3
Does the convention center sweep, not spray, parking lots, sidewalks and driveways?	1	2	3
Waste Minimization			
Does the convention center have a recycling program to recycle glass, aluminum, plastic, paper, grease and cardboard?	1	2	3
Does the convention center have a policy to reduce and reuse where possible and appropriate, and minimize paper usage?	1	2	3
Is the convention center staff trained to implement environmental policies?	1	2	3
Will the convention center work with the organization at no cost to implement a composting system, if available?	Y	N	
Environmental Purchases			
Does the convention center purchase bathroom supplies: minimum 20% recycled products for hand towels and toilet paper?	1	2	3
Does the convention center purchase environmentally responsible cleaning products for carpets, floors, kitchens and bathrooms: minimum 50% of products used to be environmentally responsible?	1	2	3
Does the convention center request vendors to have environmentally responsible practices? Does the convention center support vendors who do?	1	2	3

Hotels			
Air Quality			
Are the hotel/s located within walking distance of the convention center or easily accessible by public transportation?	Y	N	
Will the hotels provide documentation about air quality control and systems?	1	2	3
Energy Efficiency			
Do the hotels instruct staff to shut off HVAC/lights when guests are not in their rooms?	1	2	3
Water Conservation			
Are water-conservation practices such as low-flow showerheads and toilets available in hotels?	1	2	3

MeetGreen^{SM} Minimum Guidelines – Convention Center

Do the hotels offer and implement a towel and linen reuse program?	I	2	3
Waste Minimization			
Do the hotels implement a recycling program to recycle glass, aluminum, plastic, paper, grease and cardboard?	I	2	3
Do the hotels have a policy in place to reduce and reuse where possible and appropriate, and minimize paper usage?	I	2	3
Do the hotels participate in a food donation program?	I	2	3
Are hotel staffs trained to implement environmental practices?	I	2	3
Do the hotels serve food and beverage items such as juice, iced tea, coffee and water in pitchers rather than as individual servings? Do they serve condiments in bulk?	I	2	3
Will the hotels work with the organization at no cost to implement a composting system, if available?	I	2	3
Do the hotels replace unused amenities only when empty or asked by guests?	I	2	3
Do hotel food outlets ban serving food or beverages in polystyrene (Styrofoam) containers in banquet or take-out service?	I	2	3
Environmental Purchases			
Do the hotels purchase locally grown and organic foods and products wherever possible and affordable (minimum 15% of meals)?	I	2	3
Do the hotels purchase condiments and beverages in bulk?	I	2	3
Do the hotels offer sustainable menus with comparable prices?	I	2	3
Do the hotels purchase environmentally responsible bathroom supplies (minimum 20 percent recycled products for hand towels and toilet paper)?	I	2	3
Do the hotels purchase environmentally responsible cleaning products for carpets, floors, kitchens and bathrooms (minimum 50 percent of products are environmentally responsible)?	I	2	3
Do the hotels have an established program with wholesalers to utilize reusable crates or cartons?	I	2	3
Do the hotels request vendors have environmental practices in place?	I	2	3

MeetGreen^{SM} Contract Language – Convention Center

Sample language provided as a guide not intended to be construed as legal advice or documentation.

The organization (THE ORGANIZATION) is committed to conducting an environmentally responsible conference. THE CONVENTION CENTER agrees to work collaboratively with THE ORGANIZATION for the duration of this contract to ensure that the environmental performance is met.

THE CONVENTION CENTER agrees to support the commitment internally by engaging and educating all departments of THE CONVENTION CENTER regarding this commitment. THE CONVENTION CENTER will communicate to ORGANIZATION no later than 90 days before conference executes any barriers experienced for the requested environmental practices that may prevent CONVENTION CENTER from complying.

THE CONVENTION CENTER and the on-site caterer will implement the following procedures and practices during the conference.

- Minimize energy use by reducing the lights, power and HVAC during move in and move out times in the exhibit hall and turning off lights in meeting rooms when not in use.
- Minimize waste by:
  - o Providing drinking water in large containers rather than individual bottles,
  - o No Styrofoam (polystyrene #6 plastic) is to be used for any food/beverage functions or outlets,

- Provide collection bins and facilities, staffing and training necessary to recycle all glass containers, aluminum and steel cans, plastic bottles, table coverings, pallets, paper (newspaper, cardboard and other office paper), and grease.
- Conserve natural resources by purchasing and providing all paper bathroom supplies with minimum 35% post-consumer recycled content paper.
- Minimize pollution and human exposure to toxic compounds by using environmentally responsible cleaning products for carpets, floors, kitchens, and bathrooms.

MeetGreen^{SM} Contract Language – Convention Center

- Minimize air pollution by cleaning parking lots, sidewalks and driveways without the use of two-cycle combustion engines.

THE CONVENTION CENTER shall measure actual performance under each target and shall provide full documentation on the actual performance under these targets no later than <DATE>. THE CONVENTION CENTER will allow the report to be verified by an independent third party at THE ORGANIZATION'S request. THE CONVENTION CENTER shall permit THE ORGANIZATION, THE ORGANIZATION'S agent, or an independent third party access to convention center as necessary to monitor and report on all the terms of this Environmentally Responsible Meeting clause including procedures, practices and performance targets.

During ORGANIZATION'S conference, THE CONVENTION CENTER will meet or exceed the following environmental performance targets.

1. A total recycling rate of at least fifty percent (50%) of total waste.

2. CONVENTION CENTER will purchase renewable energy at a minimum of nine percent (9%) of total energy use for THE CONFERENCE.

The following specific documentation is due within 30 days or THE ORGANIZATION has the right to withhold 5% of payment due the convention center until documentation is received:

- Recycling weights/amounts for:
  - Paper, plastic, glass, aluminum/cans, cardboard

- Waste by weight for: landfill (non-recyclable materials), food
- Amount of food composted – if program has been offered
- Percentage of post-consumer recycled bathroom paper products
- Specifications of any biodegradable service products used

Optional data requested:

- Total financial contribution to local community by using local vendors

6

Transportation Selection

Participants, event supplies, food, exhibit booths and audiovisual equipment all travel to an event regardless of the efforts to choose a green destination. For the foreseeable future, most transportation methods produce carbon emissions that contribute to greenhouse gases making transportation selection a key area in minimizing a meeting's environmental impact. Does this mean we shouldn't meet? Absolutely not! Humans by nature are social creatures, and the desire for face-to-face communications has an inherent value to how we do business.

Minimizing transportation impact and working with companies to provide the most environmentally responsible transportation may never completely eliminate emissions or waste. However, measures can be taken to minimize the negative impact of transportation in the following areas: attendees, transportation vendors, ground transportation, shipping freight and carbon offsets.

FAST FACT

According to a study by the Environmental Protection Agency, the average U.S. meeting attendee, over the course of a three-day event, generates more than 80 pounds of waste and accounts for the emission of more than 1,400 pounds of greenhouse gases – the amount a typical driver produces driving a car for a month.

Influence Attendees

Most often attendees make many of their own decisions regarding transportation when coming to an event. But you have the opportunity to influence those decisions. Educate them, and provide resources so their decisions can be as environmentally responsible as possible. The following are some examples of green transportation options:

- Alert attendees to environmentally preferable transportation, such as mass transit and carpooling. Commuter trains and other mass transit systems are preferable to car travel.

- Provide information about local public transit or arrange for shuttles to transport attendees to and from the airport and the hotel or meeting venue.

- If it is available in the city, provide car-sharing for attendees who need a car for only short periods of time. Car-sharing is an excellent option for conference and event staff members who need vehicles only sporadically. Having a few bicycles to share is also a good idea.

- Provide public transit passes and maps in attendees' welcome packets.

- Provide incentives to cycle or walk to events. And allow time between events for an enjoyable walk.

- If business attire is not important, encourage casual dress so attendees feel comfortable walking or biking to events.

- Provide carbon-offset opportunities for attendees (see the Fast Facts carbon offset box for more details).

SUCCESS STORY

During a recent conference, the organizers used peer pressure to increase the number of attendees purchasing carbon credits to offset their travel. Offsets were offered for $15 per attendee and could be purchased online, at the registration counter, or at a kiosk in the exhibit hall. During the opening session, a senior manager announced the intent of the conference to offset all the travel by attendees. He said that directly after the opening session, he and other senior managers would be going to the kiosk to purchase offsets. When they did, they got a green sticker on their name badge. It didn't take long for those wanting to impress senior management to purchase their offsets as well. The organizers also had screens in front of the session rooms with the names of those who had purchased offsets scrolling throughout the day. This subtle and not-so-subtle pressure worked. As a result, this conference now holds the record for the highest attendee participation the carbon offset provider has ever seen![17]

Educate Transportation Vendors

Inform potential transportation companies of the sponsoring organization's environmental commitment and initiatives, and ask about their environmental practices. Include environmental criteria in the request for proposal and include a clause in the contract that confirms the vendor's commitment to comply with the environmental requests.

Ground Transportation

Begin by minimizing the amount and sizes of shuttle transportation as much as possible. If you have to use charter buses, consider smaller vehicles or limited routes if appropriate. For example: provide shuttle service to and from the hotel and convention venue only during peak times in the morning and afternoon. Avoid running the shuttles all day long.

Here are some questions to ask when choosing a ground transportation company:

- Do they perform environmentally responsible maintenance and recycle used oil, batteries, antifreeze and tires?
- Do they train drivers to minimize idling and the use of air conditioning, especially when no passengers are in the vehicle?
- Do they offer fuel-efficient or alternative fuel vehicles? Alternatively, are they willing to use biodiesel fuel in their existing vehicles? (Note: Diesel buses can use biodiesel fuel by changing the filters and without having to overhaul the engines.)

Shipping Freight

Consider the environmental impact when shipping event or exhibit supplies. Make sure there isn't a local source for the supplies.

When choosing a freight carrier for supplies, keep in mind the environmental impacts and ask the carrier about them, including reducing and recycling packaging. Currently, UPS is the only U.S. carrier that offers any type of environmental practices. However, the more meeting-industry professionals like you request/demand that freight companies supply alternative fuel vehicles, the more likely more companies will begin to comply. Currently, if you're shipping exhibit booths or a large quantity of event supplies, consider shipping them by rail. This is the most environmentally responsible option available. However, shipping by rail takes more time than by truck, so plan ahead.

Use the questions in the ground transportation sections of this chapter to choose a carrier.

FAST FACT – *Carbon Offsets*

To offset inevitable emissions from an event, carbon offsets are often offered on behalf of the event and participants. A carbon offset is a way of counteracting the carbon emitted when the use of fossil fuel causes greenhouse gas emissions. As you attempt to green your meetings, you'll likely hear quite a bit about carbon-offset programs and will need a basic understanding of the complicated world of carbon offsets.

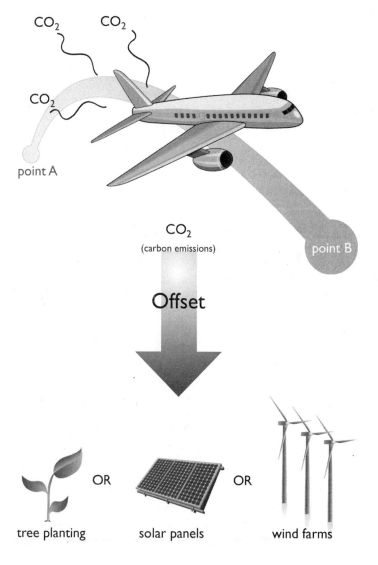

CO_2 CO_2

CO_2

point A

CO_2
(carbon emissions)

Offset

point B

tree planting   OR   solar panels   OR   wind farms

Carbon Offset Programs

Offsets commonly involve investing in projects such as renewable energy, tree planting and energy-efficiency projects. Various programs are available to calculate the emissions caused by energy use or transportation associated with your event. Resources include the Climate Trust's carbon counter (www.carboncounter.org), which is used for calculating the carbon emissions involved in travel, and the Leonardo Academy's Cleaner and Greener Event Certification program to offset most aspects of a conference (www.leonardoacademy.org).

Funding a Carbon Offset Program

There are a few scenarios for funding carbon-offset programs that meeting managers currently employ. One option is to use this program as a sponsorship opportunity and publicize that the sponsoring company has offset the entire event's greenhouse gas emissions. This strategy gains powerful recognition for both the sponsor and for the event. A second scenario is to ask attendees to offset their own travel by contributing a specific amount as part of their registration fee. Make their contribution optional. Then, those who participate will be taking an active role in contributing to improving the environment. Or include the offset as part of the conference budget and let attendees know that the organization is doing this on their behalf.

The following chart shows an example of emission offsets purchased and tracked by a conference over several years:

Pollutant Type (lbs)	2002	2003	2004	2005
Carbon dioxide (CO2)	4,660,414	5,606,214	8,096,566	9,512,121
Sulfur dioxide (SO2)	1,750	4,992	941	7,240
Nitrogen oxide (NOx)	6,144	8,007	10,149	13,423
Particulates (PM10)	990	1,251	1,964	2,133
Mercury (Hg)	0.0121	0.02346	.00166	.00310

In evaluating carbon offset programs and providers, here are some questions to consider:

- Is a carbon offset program right for the organization? Will attendees/members want the option? Is selecting one offset program too restrictive?

- What are the priorities of considering an offset program? Is the focus strictly to offset carbon emissions, or to also include other emission pollutants? Will the offset cover only travel, or other energy offsets such as hotel and convention center venues?

- Is the offset program going to be funded by sponsors, individual attendees, or both? Are you going to suggest the offset program to exhibitors?

- Is the offset to be local only, or can it benefit other areas of the country? Is the intention to have the offset program also serve as a legacy project?

- What type of carbon offsets are they (renewable energy, sequestration, donated)?

- How much of the money given to the offset provider goes toward the projects, and how much goes to pay for administration or overhead?

These questions are designed to help you and your organization be clear on why, what, how and if you want to provide offsets.

There is a lot of debate about the integrity of buying offsets and their value as a practice to minimize carbon emissions. Some believe carbon offsets are just a way of paying for sins we continue to practice, rather than a tool for having any real effect on reducing carbon. Others feel it's the best alternative we have now. The point really is to reduce first. Although travel may never be completely sustainable, it is a necessity. Currently, there is no experience that replaces the face-to-face interaction of humans at meetings and events. There are many choices planners can make with transportation to minimize its effects. So this is an area in managing a green event where it is wise to listen to Buddha's last words: "Do your best."

Test Your Knowledge

1. What two practices can you use to educate attendees about greening their transportation?

2. How do carbon offsets relate to meetings?

3. What are some environmentally friendly options to consider when hiring transportation companies?

7

Food and Beverage Selection

As individuals, we make choices every day. Paper or plastic? Window or aisle? Debit or credit? As a planner, you make choices too, for large numbers of people attending the event... beef, chicken or veggie meals? China or disposable? Local or organic? Plated or buffet?

The choices you make about food and beverages are critical to the well-being of your attendees, your budget and the planet. Food and beverage are also a very integral part of the meeting and are often tied to the social component of the meeting as well. These choices have become increasingly complicated, as attendees have come to expect food that fits their daily way of life, whether that is low-carbohydrate, organic or one of the many other options.

And to make matters more complex, many of the food choices can have a negative impact on the environment. So how do you choose what will enhance the meeting and attendee experience and still be environmentally responsible? Start by asking the food and beverage provider if they have a sustainable menu or environmentally responsible practices. There are an increasing number of providers offering such choices. Remember to include sustainable requirements in your request for proposals. Consider selecting one that does.

In the event you do not have a choice because the caterer has an exclusive arrangement with the venue or is part of a hotel, ask if they're willing to work with you. Chefs may be willing to create a menu within your budget that is more sustainable. Explain why it's important to you to serve a sustainable menu. You'll often find working with the chef gets them excited about the opportunity to do something a little different, and they can get very creative. You may find that offering sustainable choices costs more – this is one of the few areas in greening a meeting where there may be an increase in cost. However, this is also an excellent area to negotiate a reduction or to balance trade-offs.

For example:

- **Choose not to serve individual water bottles.** Serving water from large pitchers or containers saves a tremendous amount of money (US$5-10 or €4-7.50 per attendee per day depending upon the venue in the U.S.). For one conference, that was US$25,970 (€19.026) in savings over the course of the conference.[18] Additionally, it also saved all those plastic bottles from getting into the waste stream.

You can use that cost savings toward more sustainable food choices and potentially still save money overall.

Here are some ideas to make decisions easier and greener:

- **Choose food in season.** From economic, health and environmental standpoints, choosing food that is in season in the local area has great benefits. Buying locally grown products helps support the local communities and offers fresher, seasonal and regional choices without the transportation impact. It is also a great way to celebrate the local flavor of the region. From a green perspective, local and organic products are certainly the best if they are available.

- **Choose seafood from sustainable fisheries.** Increased consumer demand for seafood is depleting fish stocks around the world and harming the health of the oceans. Today, nearly 75 percent of the world's fisheries are fully fished or over-fished.[19] Two guides are available to take the guesswork out of menu selection: The Monterey Bay Aquarium publishes Seafood Watch, a guide for consumers. You can download and carry a free pocket guide (www.montereybayaquarium.org). Blue Ocean Institute publishes the Mini-Guide to Ocean Friendly Seafood. It is available for free at www.blueoceaninstitute.org.

- **Choose food based on the history of the attendees' preferences and attrition.** Planners should know the group's preferences (e.g., whether a hearty salad is plenty for them, or a full warm meal is necessary), and can order accordingly. In addition, guarantee meals based on their history. Are they early risers who all show up for breakfast, or do they arrive just before the general session, rushing in at the last minute and grabbing a cup of coffee? Do they skip the conference lunch to have smaller business meetings at local restaurants? If there is no history for the group, ask attendees to sign up for meals in advance. This will save both money and food.

Not only do you make choices about the food and beverages served, but also about how it is served. How food is served can also have a tremendous impact on the environment. For example:

Choose china service.
Disposable cups, plates and flatware not only add to landfills, they also

don't deliver the same "first-class" service experience. The Environmental Defense Council reports, "Using 1,000 disposable plastic teaspoons consumes over 10 times more energy and natural resources than manufacturing one stainless steel teaspoon and washing it 1,000 times." 20 Using cloth instead of paper napkins also adds to the experience.

If disposables must be used, be sure they are biodegradable or can be composted. Avoid using the popular black plasticware so many caterers use. That plastic has the same makeup as polystyrene (the stuff Styrofoam is made of) and is toxic to produce and toxic to destroy, and some studies are finding that it emits toxins when heated.

Using an alternative to the black plastic may even save money. Recently, we asked a caterer to use an alternative, earth-friendly product instead of black plastic. The caterer originally was going to charge the client more; however, it turned out that the biodegradable product ordered was actually $2,700 (€1.947) less!

When we "greened" the Live Earth concert in Giants Stadium, using china service for 51,000 fans would have been impossible. Think of the amount of hot dogs, pizza slices, pretzels, etc. they went through during the eight-hour concert! What we were able to do, however, was convince the stadium caterer to use biodegradable cups, wrappers, cutlery, etc. Because we had composting available for the event, these items were then thrown into the compost bins along with the leftover food items, avoiding food waste going into the landfill waste.

FAST FACT

According to the Oregon Food Bank, one in five people in Oregon and southwestern Washington state (total population approximately 4 million people) eats donated food at least once a year. Thirty-eight percent of these people are children. Most likely, the statistics are similar in most communities. Donating leftover food from conferences and events is an important component of social responsibility.

Reduce Waste

Write a clause into the contract requiring the hotel or caterer to donate leftover food, and request they start an ongoing program. This is a wonderful legacy to leave behind.

Be prepared if a caterer says that donating food is against the health code. First explain to them about the Good Samaritan Law that protects anyone from donating food in good faith from being sued. (Find the full text of the Good Samaritan Law at http://www.usda.gov/news/pubs/gleaning/appc.htm). Each major city in the U.S. has some type of food-donation facility.

Secondly, explain that the idea is for them to work with a local food donation outlet to ensure food is protected in a way that makes it possible to donate. For example: If plated meals are kept in the hot boxes in the kitchen until served, any unused meals can be donated if they have not been held too long. Also, items for a buffet that have not been put out on the buffet should be able to be donated. Again, it's important to work with a local food donation outlet, because they will have their own set of guidelines.

A good deal of the food and beverage waste is in both the packaging and the serving. The following are tips for reducing this waste:

Purchasing and Packaging
- Purchase organic and/or local products whenever possible.
- Request minimal packaging on all food products.
- Purchase environmentally responsible cleaning products. A list of Green Seal Certified cleaning products can be found at www.greenseal.org.

Serving
- Eliminate or minimize the use of forest-based and petroleum-based products, such as paper plates and plastic eating utensils.
- Do not allow polystyrene products to be used.
- Use cloth instead of paper napkins. If cloth is not available, use recyclable napkins with a high post-consumer content.
- Use china and glassware. If they are not available, use biodegradable, disposable serviceware in conjunction with a composting program.
- Serve condiments, spreads and jams in bowls (or appropriate containers) rather than in individually wrapped packages.
- Serve water and juice in pitchers, and soft drinks in returnable containers.
- Consider using reusable beverage containers. Consider offering a conference mug and stock corporate meeting spaces with glassware.
- Do not pre-fill drinking water; serve it upon request at banquets.
- Eliminate the use of boxes for lunches. Use reusable containers, fabric lunch bags or picnic baskets.

- Minimize the use of tablecloths, especially for layering.
- Table decorations can include live, potted flowers or plants, a bowl of fruit or a special dessert on a pedestal.
- Provide signage that tells attendees whether food is locally grown, organic or seasonal.

Non-sustainable	Sustainable
individual plastic water bottle	pitcher and glasses or compostable cups
individual serving packets (sugar, jam, etc.)	bulk containers
black plastic #6, styrofoam, plastic utensils	chinaware, metal flatware
exotic cut flower centerpiece	living plant centerpiece

Some examples of non-sustainable and sustainable food and beverage options.

FAST FACT

For a three-day event serving 4,200 attendees, not pre-filling water glasses and not using saucers saved:
- -520 gallons (1968 liters) of drinking water
- -12,400 gallons (46.939 liters) of dishwater[7]

Reduce, Reuse and Recycle

- The venue and caterer should recycle paper, glass, plastics, cans, aluminum, corrugated boxes and kitchen grease.
- Provide recycling bins for paper, bottles and cans. Ensure the bins are actually used for recycling. If the facility does not have recycling capability, contract with an independent hauler to provide and remove recycling bins.
- Food and food-contaminated paper waste should be composted.

As with most of the green practices described in this manual, the food and beverage practices are mostly cost-saving or cost-neutral. The exception is in requesting locally grown, organic food. Depending on the amount of food being ordered, the location of the meeting, the time of year and what is local, providing locally grown, organic food may cost more. Negotiate with the food and beverage provider in the beginning to see if any concessions can be made for the event. Engage the chef in these conversations. Chefs often will be creative and provide lower-cost options than what's presented on the standard menus.

Remember to include in the contract the green meeting practices that the food and beverage provider agreed to implement. Be sure the environmental expectations are listed and that the method of measurement is clearly defined.

One final note here before you test your knowledge. We quite often get "push back" from event organizers and venues alike, saying they want a high level of service for their guests and that green practices just aren't appropriate. We strongly disagree! Usually the green practices increase the perceived level of service. Wouldn't we all rather eat on china instead of a paper plate? And when we sit down to a banquet to find a water glass that hasn't been pre-filled and sitting there for a while, isn't it nice to have a server come and offer to pour us a glass of water? These are just a couple of examples; I'm sure you can think of more.

The following pages include a green meeting minimum guideline document and sample contract language.

Test Your Knowledge

1. List at least five environmentally responsible practices to request for food and beverage.

2. If you had to pick three green requests, which would those be?

3. What are some options in choosing food and beverages to make meal functions less harmful to the environment and benefit the community?

MeetGreen^{SM} Minimum Guidelines – Caterer

Conference: **Conference Dates:**
City for Consideration:

The intended result of requiring MeetGreen^{SM} Strategies is to support the mission and values of <ORGANIZATION NAME> by practicing sustainable, responsible meeting management strategies. <ORGANIZATION NAME> is taking the opportunity to strengthen green meeting management practices by driving the meeting and convention market to adopt environmentally responsible practices. The green strategies are customized for the <CONFERENCE NAME> and are categorized in the following five areas: air quality, energy efficiency, water conservation, waste minimization and environmental purchasing. These strategies focus primarily on site selection; a more complete set of guidelines will be presented further into the planning process.

Please note: MeetGreen^{SM} Strategies should be offered at no additional cost to the organization.   Preference will be given to sites with a maximum number of policies/practices in place. These strategies serve as minimally expected practices. Additional detailed strategies may be required. Compliance language to ensure implementation will be included in the final contract.

Please complete the following survey questions, indicating the level of green practices. Circle the number or statement according to the following key:	
1	Currently available and/or implemented
2	Will commit to implementation in time for the start of conference/event.
3	Currently not available, and no future plans to implement

MeetGreen^{SM} Minimum Guidelines – Caterer

Caterer			
Water Conservation			
Does the caterer implement water-saving strategies (for example, not pre-filling water glasses, not providing saucers under coffee cups or offering large containers of drinking water rather than individual bottles)?	1	2	3
Does the caterer reduce the use of ice in drinking water?	1	2	3
Waste Minimization			
Does the caterer implement a recycling program to recycle glass, aluminum, plastic, paper, grease and cardboard?	1	2	3
Does the caterer have a policy in place to reduce and reuse where possible and appropriate, and minimize paper usage?	1	2	3
Does the caterer donate leftover food?	1	2	3
Is the catering staff trained to implement environmental policies?	1	2	3
Does the caterer serve juice, iced tea, coffee and water in pitchers and serve condiments in bulk?	1	2	3
Does the caterer use china service (or, if not possible, use biodegradable disposable serviceware)?	1	2	3
Will the caterer work with the organization at no cost to implement a composting system if available?	1	2	3
Environmental Purchases			
Does the caterer purchase locally grown and organic foods and products wherever possible and affordable (minimum 20 percent of meals)?	1	2	3
Does the caterer purchase condiments and beverages in bulk?	1	2	3
Does the caterer offer sustainable menus with comparable prices?	1	2	3

MeetGreen^{SM} Contract Language – Caterer

Sample language provided as a guide – not intended to be construed as legal advice or documentation.

The organization (ORGANIZATION) is committed to conducting an environmentally responsible conference. The caterer (CATERER) agrees to support that goal through environmentally responsible procedures and practices of CATERER and its employees, vendors and contractors. CATERER agrees to work collaboratively with ORGANIZATION for the duration of this contract to ensure that the environmental performance goals are met.

CATERER agrees to support the commitment internally by engaging and educating all departments of CATERER regarding this commitment. CATERER will communicate to ORGANIZATION no later than 90 days before conference begins any barriers experienced for the requested environmental practices that may prevent CATERER from complying.

Environmental Expectations
CATERER will implement the following procedures and practices during the conference at no additional cost to ORGANIZATION.

Waste Minimization –

- Serving juice, ice tea, coffee and water in pitchers rather than individual containers (if this service is provided by the caterer).
- Using china service or biodegradable disposable serviceware rather than paper or plastic serviceware at no additional cost to ORGANIZATION, unless china service is used during catered functions that are reception-style meals served in exhibit halls. If a sit-down meal is served in an exhibit hall no additional costs will be charged to ORGANIZATION for china service.
- NO polystyrene (#6 plastic) used under any circumstances.
- Serve condiments in bulk containers, not individual servings. This includes sugar, creamer, butter, cream cheese, etc. (exception: serve sugar substitutes in individual servings).
- Use cloth napkins whenever possible. Use coasters instead of cocktail napkins. If paper napkins are required, they must be made of post-

MeetGreen^{SM} Contract Language – Caterer

consumer recycled paper.

- Donate all leftover food to the degree possible within safety and health regulations and   Good Samaritan laws.
- Compost all table scraps or donate them to a local farm, if a program is available or arranged for by ORGANIZATION.
- Provide sustainable food, as defined below:
    - o   First preference – local and organic/natural
    - o   Second preference – local, non-organic
    - o   Third preference – organic, non-local
    - o   Local defined as a product grown within 500 miles
    - o   CATERER agrees to provide at least 20 percent of the portion served at catered functions as sustainable food, at no additional cost to ORGANIZATION.
    - o   Concessions: CATERER agrees that 25 percent of the concession menu offered will feature sustainable food options and be priced accordingly.

Recycling Participation – CATERER is to provide collection bins and facilities, as well as staffing and training necessary to recycle all glass containers, aluminum and steel cans, plastic bottles, table coverings, paper (newspaper, cardboard and other office paper) and grease.

Environmentally Responsible Paper Products – Conserve natural resources by purchasing and providing   all paper supplies with the highest post-consumer recycled content available.

Environmentally Responsible Cleaning Products – Minimize pollution and human exposure to toxic compounds by using environmentally responsible cleaning products for kitchens.

Food and Food Products – Support local and sustainable agriculture by purchasing food and food   products that are fresh and locally grown or certified as sustainable grown or organic – wherever possible and economically feasible – and offer sustainable menu options reflecting the real

MeetGreen^{SM} Contract Language – Caterer

costs of purchases. Provide a minimum average of 15 percent of total weight in food served as sustainable and organic, at regular menu prices.

In the event a food composting option is not sponsored or offered by the city, then CATERER shall work with ORGANIZATION to implement food composting for the event at no additional costs to ORGANIZATION. (Food composting will include prep food, table scraps and all food items.)

CATERER shall permit ORGANIZATION, ORGANIZATION's agent or an independent third party access to the catering practices as necessary to monitor and report on all the terms of this Environmentally Responsible Meeting clause, including procedures, practices and performance targets.

The following specific documentation is due within 30 days after the event in order to receive any final payment due CATERER:

- Recycling weights/amounts for: Paper, plastic, glass, aluminum/cans, cardboard
- Waste, by weight, for: landfill (non-recyclable materials), food
- Amount of donated food in weight
- Food, in weight, that was composted
- Percentage of locally grown products used in food/beverage services
- Percentage of organically grown products used in food/beverage services
- Percentage of post-consumer recycled paper products
- Specifications of any biodegradable service products used

Optional data requested:

- Potential water savings by not pre-filling for any meal functions
- Total financial contribution to local community by using local vendors

Exhibition Production

8

If you've ever been on a trade show floor an hour after the show closes, you've seen the amount of waste on the floor. There is paper, cardboard, all sorts of giveaways, flower arrangements, lumber... you name it. We even saw a Koi fish once after a home and garden show. Trade shows and expositions are often the components of a conference or event that have the most significant impact on the environment. Exhibitions use large amounts of energy, require considerable transportation and generate a tremendous amount of waste – all of which affect air quality. So this is a very important aspect of green events.

Make Smart Choices

Exhibitions offer a tremendous opportunity to minimize their negative environmental impact through the choices made by the organizers, facility, general services contractor and exhibitors. Collaboration among these players is crucial to creating an environmentally responsible exhibition or trade show. You will most likely be setting the stage for such collaboration. Make sure to include environmental expectations in the request for proposals and subsequently in the contracts with all these players.

FAST FACT

A three-day conference with 496 exhibit booths and 8,100 attendees can consume more than 617,000 kilowatt hours of electricity, more than 28,000 therms of natural gas, and more than 376,000 gallons (1,423,315 liters) of fuel. Additionally, it is estimated that for a meeting of this size, more than 8 million tons (7,257,478 metric tons) of carbon is emitted into the air.[7] This example represents only one exhibition held in the United States. Imagine how many are produced daily worldwide!

Begin with the venue where the exhibition is being held. The venue plays a crucial role in the ability to implement environmental practices. For example, if the venue does not have a recycling program in place, minimizing the impact of waste will be much more difficult. The facility will also need to work with exhibitors to minimize energy use during move-in and move-out.

Here are some basic environmentally responsible practices the facility should provide:

- Recycle bins on the show floor. Many facilities that have recycling programs do not tend to ensure recycling bins are placed on the show floor during move-in and move-out and during the show. Make sure that recycling bins are placed next to trash receptacles, not across the aisle or against an adjacent wall.

- Collection bins for less common materials (batteries, vinyl table coverings), especially during move-in and move-out.

- Information for exhibitors outlining what material is collected and what they must do to participate.

- An area to donate leftover signage, giveaways and flowers to schools or civic organizations. This is something that will also have to be coordinated with the general services contractor/decorator.

- Organization names to contact for the donated items. Your organization may have a donation stream in place, or the facility maybe able to recommend one. Depending on the timing of leftovers, schools, churches, theatres and community nonprofits can be good resources.

- Lighting and electrical conservation practices using half-lights and no HVAC during move-in and move-out.

Once the facility is onboard, be sure the general services contractor has agreed to support and participate in the environmental practices. At a minimum the general services contractor should do the following:

- Use recycled, recyclable and/or environmentally responsibly cleaned trade show materials (e.g., drapes, carpets).

- Use recyclable or biodegradable shipping and packing materials, such as paper and corrugated boxes instead of polystyrene and plastic wrap, and reuse whenever possible.

- Coordinate with the planning organization, exhibitors and facility to collect donated items. The general service contractor will need to provide the location and type of donation items being collected and how and when the exhibitors are to donate them.

- Provide carbon-offset programs for shipping and freight. You may want to refer to Chapter 6, Transportation Selection, for more information about carbon offsets.

There also environmental expectations for the exhibitors and exhibiting companies. Make sure you include any environmental criteria in the rules and regulations exhibitors must sign, as well as in a cover letter if the criteria are new to them.

Exhibitors should be asked to adhere to the following guidelines:

- Use soy-based ink and post-consumer recycled paper to produce materials.
- Use recycled or consumable products as giveaways.
- Do not have gift items made from endangered or threatened species.
- Avoid bringing large quantities of collateral materials – send them upon request instead.
- Trade show booths should be made from sustainable or reusable materials and/or designed as environmentally consciously as possible.
- Minimize packaging materials and/or use recyclable or biodegradable shipping and packing materials.
- Purchase supplies that have minimal packaging.
- Assist the move-in/-out process by recycling cardboard, freight boxes and plastic wrap.

Sustainable giveaways

pencils made from reclaimed wood

mousepad made with recycled rubber

cornstarch mugs

organic chocolates

FAST FACT

Some organizations have designed awards to encourage exhibitors to participate in these practices. At Greenbuild International Conference and Trade Show, they have an award program for exhibitors. Exhibitors can participate in the award process by filling out the online award criteria and nominating their company. A team of judges verifies the criteria and awards points according to the number of criteria met. Those with the highest number of points go into a drawing for a free booth for the following year.

Once the facility, general services contractor and exhibitor are on track, the responsibility of you and the sponsor organization is to provide:

- Accurate expected attendance numbers so exhibitors can bring the corresponding number of materials for distributing, thereby cutting down on waste.

- Electronic scan cards for attendee profiles.

- An avenue for donated items. For example: schools or other charitable organizations can be a great place to donate leftover pens, paper, foam core signs or conference bags.

- A clause in the agreement with the facility and/or general services contractor to:
    - o Provide recycling services for cardboard, pallets, paper, cans, plastic, glass and other recyclable materials that are generated; also provide trained clean-up crews who will keep recyclable and reusable items out of the garbage.
    - o Specific environmental practices requested.
    - o Measured results of recycling materials and waste, plus any water or energy conversation data available.

- A clause in the exhibitor agreement to comply with the following:
    - o Minimize the use of collateral materials and, for any necessary materials, request they are produced on post-consumer paper stock, using vegetable-based inks.
    - o Minimize their packaging and participate in recycling packaging when appropriate.
    - o Use recycled or consumable products as giveaways when possible and do not use gift items made from endangered or threatened species. In addition, attempt to use locally grown/made products.

- Name badges printed on recycled paper using recycled name badge holders, making sure they are recycled, too.
- Conference bags made of recycled or sustainable materials.
- Programs printed on 100% post-consumer recycled paper with soy-based ink.

FAST FACT

Remember, donations do not have to be fancy or in large quantities – every bit helps. One of our clients had a goal to have a positive impact on the community. Exhibitors from their conference donated the following supplies to a local organization:
- *Four bundles of insulation*
- *100 linear feet of padding*
- *200 linear feet of carpet*
- *100 square feet of rooftop garden materials*
- *Three boxes of giveaways to a local community storehouse[7]*

As you can see, maximizing the potential for greening an exhibit show takes the collaboration of all the stakeholders. The more committed the players are to minimizing the environmental footprint, the more likely you are to be successful. Track and measure what was accomplished. For example: What percentage of exhibitors used the online kits versus having the kits mailed? Track what types of items were donated, and how much of each. You can use this information post-event for marketing.

Though trade shows have a tremendous impact on the environment, it's up to you and your team whether the impact will be positive or negative. Whatever practices you employ, be sure to let attendees know what's been done to minimize the environmental footprint. Ask them for feedback and suggestions. This could be the most talked-about exhibit show you've ever done.

The following two pages offer sample environmental contract language documents for the decorator/general service contractor and the exhibitor.

Test Your Knowledge

1. What three green meeting practices will you include in the exhibitor rules and regulations?

2. What three green meeting practices will you include in the decorator/ general services contractor agreement?

3. What can exhibitors do to minimize their impact on the environment?

MeetGreen^{SM} Contract Language – General Services Contractor

Sample language provided as a guide – not intended to be construed as legal advice or documentation. (For purposes of this document, General Services Contractor is the equivalent of a decorator.)

SHOW MANAGEMENT is committed to conducting an environmentally responsible meeting. GENERAL SERVICES CONTRACTOR agrees to support that goal through environmentally responsible procedures and practices of its services and its employees, vendors and contractors. GENERAL SERVICES CONTRACTOR agrees to work collaboratively with SHOW MANAGEMENT for the duration of this contract to improve the overall environmental performance and efficiency of the GENERAL SERVICES CONTRACTOR services. GENERAL SERVICES CONTRACTOR agrees to support the commitment internally by engaging and educating all departments of the GENERAL SERVICES CONTRACTOR of this special commitment.

GENERAL SERVICES CONTRACTOR will implement the following procedures and practices during the conference.

- Minimize Energy Use – Reducing the lights, power and HVAC during move-in and move-out times in the exhibit hall.

- Exhibitor Kits/Service – Kits will be available electronically via the Web site. Any binders that are mailed to exhibitors will be made from 35 percent post-consumer recovered fiber and recycled paper. The contents of the binder will be printed on post-consumer recycled paper, with vegetable-based inks.

- Tabletop Coverings – Coverings will be tabletop vinyl pre-cut to length, and wooden tables and biodegradable trash can liners will be used.

- Booth Headers – Should be made from renewable forest byproducts with water-based ink.

- Aisle Signs/Show Signage /Double-sided Signs, Graphics and Logos – Use products made of environmentally responsible components with applied and removable water-based graphics.

- Information Signage – Use a recyclable board or alternative environmentally responsible product.

- Registration Counter/Kiosks – Use lighting that is Energy Star Saver-approved with T-8 ballast and bulbs – using 30 percent less energy.

MeetGreen^{SM} Contract Language – General Services Contractor

Counters are to be re-usable, and graphics and logo should be re-usable.

- Magazine Bins – Use re-usable bins. Logos will be printed with water-based inks. The shelves should be made of renewable resources or certified forest products and may not contain tropical hardwoods or endangered wood species.

- Booth and Aisle Carpet – Use carpet made from recycled materials and fully recyclable itself.

- Equipment – Use natural gas forklifts and hand carts to move exhibitor freight in and out of the show, to assist in the air quality.

- Shipping and Packing Materials – Make biodegradable shipping and packing materials available to exhibitors and show management.

- Transportation – Reduce the environmental impact resulting from transportation while supporting the regional economy. Partner with a local contractor to manage and use local labor. Minimize transportation to and from the show site. Use biodiesel-fueled or alternative fuel trucks. Offset transportation emissions with a carbon offset program.

- Donation area – GENERAL SERVICES CONTRACTOR will provide and manage a donation area for exhibitors/SHOW MANAGEMENT to collect donated items. GENERAL SERVICES CONTRACTOR will work with the local organizations collecting the items.

- Staff Training – Staff will be trained to assist the facility with properly disposing of recyclable materials and other waste. Personnel will be informed about the environmentally responsible practices to be implemented during this show.

GENERAL SERVICES CONTRACTOR shall permit SHOW MANAGEMENT, SHOW MANAGEMENT's agent or an independent third party access to GENERAL SERVICES CONTRACTOR General Services Contractor services as necessary to monitor and report on all the terms of this Environmentally Responsible Meeting clause, including procedures, practices and performance targets.

MeetGreen^{SM} Contract Language – General Services Contractor

The following specific documentation is due within 30 days after the event to receive ten percent of the final payment due to the GENERAL SERVICES CONTRACTOR:

- Detailed specifics on types of materials used in each category listed above
- Description of vehicles used and fuel sources
- Amount of items donated
- Number of exhibitor kits mailed versus sent electronically

MeetGreen^{SM} Contract Language – Exhibitor

Sample language provided as a guide – not intended to be construed as legal advice or documentation.

SHOW MANAGEMENT is committed to conducting an environmentally responsible meeting. EXHIBITOR agrees to support that goal through environmentally responsible procedures and practices of its services and its employees, vendors and contractors. EXHIBITOR agrees to work collaboratively with SHOW MANAGEMENT for the duration of this contract to improve the overall environmental performance of the EXHIBITOR. Similarly, EXHIBITOR agrees to support the commitment internally by engaging and educating all departments of the EXHIBITOR services of this special commitment.

EXHIBITOR will implement the following procedures and practices during the conference.

- Recycling Participation – Exhibitors will participate in the facility's recycling efforts by ensuring they recycle cardboard, freight boxes and plastic wrappings, and other recyclable items during move-in and move-out.

- Minimize Packaging Materials – Exhibitors will make a conscious effort to minimize packing materials.

- Environmentally Responsible Packing Materials – Exhibitors are to use recyclable, biodegradable shipping and packing materials or environmentally responsible alternatives.

- Avoid Large Quantities of Collateral – Bring samples or small amounts of materials and offer to send information upon request. Avoid dated material.

- Printed Materials – Printed materials must use soy/vegetable-based ink and post-consumer, recycled paper (minimum 30 percent).

- Environmentally Responsible Giveaways – Giveaways should be made of recycled, responsibly grown natural fiber, be non-toxic and biodegradable, and be useful, not merely promotional in nature. Any food (candy, etc.) should be sustainably grown, processed and packaged.

- Gift Items Made from Endangered or Threatened Species – These items are NOT allowed.

MeetGreen^{SM} Contract Language – Exhibitor

- Design and Displays – Both should incorporate indoor air quality principals and be made with environmentally responsible materials and include energy-efficient lighting if applicable.

- Signage – Must be reusable, made of recycled materials or donated.

- Transportation – Reduce the environmental impact resulting from transportation while supporting the regional economy. Partner with a local contractor to manage and use local labor. Minimize transportation to and from the show site. Use biodiesel-fueled or alternative fuel trucks. Offset transportation emissions with a carbon offset program.

- Staff Training – Staff will be trained to assist facility with properly disposing of recyclable materials and other waste. Personnel will be informed about the environmentally responsible practices to be implemented during this show.

- Donations – An area will be provided to collect any materials that are eligible for donation.

EXHIBITOR shall permit SHOW MANAGEMENT, SHOW MANAGEMENT's agent or an independent third party access to EXHIBITOR services/products as necessary to monitor and report on all the terms of this Environmentally Responsible Meeting clause, including procedures, practices and performance.

To be included in the final case study produced following the show, please provide the following specific documentation, due within 30 days after the event:

- Detailed specifics on types of materials used in each category listed above

- Type and amount of items donated

CHAPTER

Communications and Marketing **9**

Communications and marketing are not just about the paper, ink and electronic methods used. They are about creating awareness and building understanding. They are about sharing with the media, employees, attendees, stakeholders and the world the difference you, the planner, are making by planning the event in an environmentally and socially responsible way.

Spread the Word

Share your efforts with everyone. This point is often overlooked, but it is vital to the continued success of a green program. Tell the sponsoring organization's board, the membership, meeting attendees, the press, peers and clients. Communicate all environmentally responsible efforts in all promotional materials, including press releases, conference programs and Web sites.

Publishing the green practices of events in a case study with quantifiable results is an excellent marketing piece for the conference and sponsoring organization. Post it on the conference Web site for all to review. You should share data with professional associates; they will be interested in what efforts were made, how they were accomplished, and what outcomes were achieved. Networking with other planners who employ green meeting practices is important as well.

You can submit a press release or write an article for your organizational newsletter, industry trade publication or local media. Include statistics and quotes from attendees on how their participation in a green meeting affected the quality of their experience.

Apply for an award. There are award programs for green management in the environmental and social arenas as well as from meeting management organizations. These awards showcase the exciting new innovations in green meeting practices.

RESOURCE

IMEX, in partnership with the Green Meeting Industry Council, presents the only awards currently recognizing green efforts for meetings, exhibitors and suppliers. Full details, including deadlines for submissions, can be found at IMEX Green Awards: www.imex-frankfurt.com/greenawards.html

The following are communication and marketing ideas that engage and involve attendees:

- Appoint recycling advisors to assist attendees; give attendees a prize when caught doing something right.
- Provide walking and public transportation maps so attendees can visit the city without renting a car.
- Suggest attendees take full advantage of the hotel's commitment to reuse linens and participate in their recycling programs, and also turn off lights. Suggest they pass on the daily paper unless they intend to read and recycle it. Also encourage attendees not to order room service or take-out.
- Ask attendees to bring their favorite water bottle and coffee cup from home.
- Provide a list of suggestions for attendees to continue their efforts back home. Make the list available on the conference Web site or through confirmation or follow-up e-mails.
- Put greening statistics up on the screen during the walk-in to a general session You can even have a trivia contest later. Give a prize to the attendees who know the most statistics.
- Include questions about the event's environmental stewardship in the formal evaluation, and solicit attendees' suggestions on how to build on the success.

The event's communication materials should also demonstrate the organization's commitment to environmental responsibility. For the more formal communication involved with a conference, the following green practices are recommended:

- Reduce paper usage by using the Web and e-mail lists to promote events. Publish the registration brochure online.
- If a flyer needs to be mailed, use post-consumer content, chlorine-free paper printed on both sides with vegetable-based inks.
- Send media and sponsorship packets electronically.

- Conduct all conference correspondence via e-mail.
- Encourage online registration and send confirmation e-mails to attendees.
- Consider not providing a conference bag. If one is provided, make sure attendees have the option to not take one, and let them know it will be donated on their behalf. Also, ensure the bag is made from eco-friendly materials.
- Limit sponsor handouts for the bags or print all sponsor information in a newsletter format that is produced in an eco-friendly way.
- Consider making the final program available online instead of on paper.
- Ask hotels for electronic check-in/check-out services. All correspondence with hotels should be electronic, including BEOs.

Reusable signs minimize printing from year to year, saving money and resources.

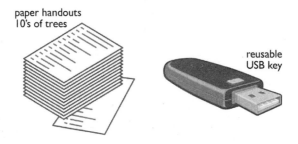

Instead of using trees and resources for paper handouts that will be thrown away, offer reusable USB keys that attendees will keep long after your event.

FAST FACTS

One of our clients improved the use of their Web site for post-conference and presentation materials as a way of curbing paper consumption.
They also communicated with delegates using online methods wherever possible, eliminating all pre-conference printed mailings.

Another client eliminated handouts for a two-day, 1,300-person conference, saving nearly US$2,000 (€1.475) in printing costs.

The following page illustrates a condensed version of a case study. This particular conference won the IMEX Environmental Meetings Award – Silver level – in recognition of its achievements.

Test Your Knowledge

1. List at least three practices that would reduce, reuse and/or recycle.

2. What three green practices can you ask attendees to do? When should you ask them?

3. Using more technology (such as online registration, online exhibitor kits and an electronic brochure) reduces which of the following?

    a) Paper
    b) Electricity
    c) Costs
    d) a and c
    e) All of the above

2005 Case Study

Sierra Summit 2005

The Sierra Club's National Environmental Convention and Expo

BACKGROUND AND INTRODUCTION

Nearly 4,000 attendees and 148 exhibiting companies (200 booths) from across the nation participated in the inaugural Sierra Summit 2005, produced by the Sierra Club, America's oldest, largest and most influential grass-roots environmental organization. The four-day meeting was held in the club's birthplace, San Francisco, on September 8-11, 2005. The Sierra Club's interest in creating a "green" event was understandable and absolutely expected.

PARTNERS IN GREEN

As the green consultant, Meeting Strategies Worldwide began by reviewing the environmental policies and systems of each of the participating facilities and vendors. The Moscone Center, the local venue, worked with us to ensure the conference would maximize their current system structure to reduce landfill waste. Next, we met with and relayed to the vendors the Sierra Club's environmental expectations, opening a dialog for minimizing environmental impact.

HOW GREEN WAS IT?

Requesting that environmental practices be implemented was the first step. The next step was to ensure the practices agreed upon were included in the contracts. Measuring the environmental components was the third step in evaluating the success of greening the conference.

Recycling

According to figures from the Moscone Center, the following materials were recycled:

An estimated one bale of cardboard (bag stuffing, kitchen and exhibits)	2,000 lbs
Mixed paper (actual weight)	4,200 lbs
Can and bottles (estimated 1/4 of total)	490 lbs
Exhibitor wood chips and leftover wood	500 lbs
Exhibitor food donation (actual weight)	562 lbs
Compost (two 4-yard bins – estimated)	6,000 lbs
Pallets for reuse	500 pallets

Results: An estimated 80 percent of waste was diverted, not including food donation from SMG, the facility's caterer. Only 2,780 pounds of garbage went to the landfill.

Food and Beverage

SMG put together a menu healthier than its usual offerings. In addition, the company didn't use polystyrene or black plastic to-go containers. The caterer:

- Arranged for 200 lbs of consumable, leftover food to be donated.
- Served 300 vegetarian/vegan meals.
- Served Sierra Club fair trade/shade-grown coffee.
- Served approximately 30 to 50 percent local and/or organic food.

The only product not recyclable or able to be composted was the chip bags sold at the concessions.

Marketing, Communication and Registration

It was a given that attendees expected the conference to be green. Some of the highlights for communication were:

- Soy-based inks and the paper with the highest percentage of post-consumer recycled paper were used for all printed materials, including the program.
- Signage used was donated post-event to a local school.
- Recycled name badge holders were used, then turned in to be recycled again.

LESSONS LEARNED

As with every project, there were opportunities to learn from the experience. The following lessons are shared with the intention to educate and motivate others to take on greening their events.

1. Know your community and its infrastructure. Contact local EPA regarding rules and resources. Make sure waste management is in place; otherwise you'll be asking for things that can't be achieved. Research local laws.
2. Even with solid environmental practices in place, new ideas and products should be considered to continue to improve practices.
3. Start the greening process with site selection. This allows you to minimize travel required and to choose a facility that has environmental management systems already in place.

CONCLUSION

The greening of the Sierra Summit in San Francisco was successful in a number of ways. In the short term, the conference minimized its impact on the local ecosystem. Long-term, it raised awareness and educated venues, vendors and attendees. Because every event that identifies environmental stewardship as a priority is a step in the right direction, the Sierra Club is now part of the growing number of organizations illustrating how all gatherings, regardless of whether they involve industry, nonprofits or religious organizations can be more environmentally responsible.

On-site Office Procedures 10

You may be recycling at the office, but what about at the conference or event? Even better, you may be recycling and using both sides of the paper for printing, but are you reducing the number of copies you need? This is where you lead by example, in the event and registration offices. The command base for green event management should exemplify the principles of environmental responsibility.

The following practices are intended to apply to an on-site office at a conference or event. While these recommendations are not comprehensive, nor do they consider all aspects of a work space, they can be applied directly to any work environment. Make sure your on-site staff and volunteers are well-versed in the greening aspects of the meeting.

FAST FACTS

 One conference went to extreme lengths to eliminate paper waste. In one year they eliminated approximately 250,000 printed items, such as envelopes, mailers and written correspondence, saving the equivalent of 30 trees. They also managed to use only 500 sheets of letterhead, compared with 10,000 sheets at their previous conference.[17]

So not only did they save the actual trees, they also mitigated the environmental impact of processing the paper and mailing items. They also realized significant savings by not having to purchase the extra paper products or spend for printing services.

Implement the Practices

Whether in the office at work or at an event, energy-efficient equipment provides both cost and environmental savings.

Equipment and Supplies
- Purchase/rent Energy Star™ or energy-efficient products.
- When purchasing/renting laser printers, choose a model that reduces energy consumption when idle.

- Consider using a laptop computer. On average laptops use 10 percent or less of the energy consumed by desktop computers.
- Buy recharged toner cartridges and recycled ink cartridges for printers or copy machines.
- Choose copy machines that can duplex all documents. Look for a machine that can also handle multiple functions such as faxing and printing.
- Encourage employees to turn off equipment and lighting and turn down thermostats when leaving for extended periods of time.
- Bring your own water bottle and coffee mug.

Communications
- Use e-mail communications whenever possible.
- When e-mailing is not possible, make double-sided copies using paper with at least 30 percent post-consumer recycled content.
- Ask attendees to sign up for handouts or proceedings.
- Make sure e-mail and mailing lists are kept up-to-date.
- Use signage that can be reused whenever possible. Directional signage can be used with different clients and organizations. Signage from the same organization can be used again if the year and destination do not appear. The exhibit decorator can store large items like the kick panels for registration counters or meter signs. Just ask! It is in their best interest, because if they have your signs stored, chances are you will be using the decorator again.
- Use the hotel's in-room television station to publish information.
- Ask for recycled paper flip charts.

Recycling
- Make sure to use the facility's recycling systems to recover cardboard, paper, glass, cans, glass, batteries and toner cartridges.
- Donate all leftover supplies (including conference bags) to a local school or day care.

Test Your Knowledge

1. What can you do at your next event to green your onsite office?
2. Who needs to be aware of the green on-site office procedures?

Summary

So there you have it – green meeting practices as we know them today.

At the beginning of this book, we mentioned GE's initiative to take on environmental stewardship. Since starting their environmental campaign in 2005, GE has reported enormous success. They have doubled their sales of environmentally friendly products and services to $12 billion in revenues in just two years. As noted in their 2006 Ecomagination Report, GE "has never had an initiative that has generated better financial returns so quickly."

So much change and evolution are occurring every day in the meetings industry in relation to green practices. As mentioned in the beginning of this book, green meeting standards are being created worldwide. The path – or, rather, push – to be green may look different to each of us. However, it's no longer if you decide to incorporate green practices; it's when. Your ability to implement these practices will put you at the cutting edge of event management and increase your value to an organization.

The added benefit to planning environmental meetings is that they can save organizations money while reducing their impact on the environment. Quantifying the costs savings will also increase the demand and participation of green meeting practices. This is just the beginning to what will be possible in the future.

We hope our experiences and ideas are helpful as you begin your own journey. Remember the myths we talked about, and don't let them stop you. Green meetings are NOT:

- Expensive
- More work
- Only for "environmental types"
- Required to be 100 percent to make a difference. Just start somewhere.

Start anywhere in the process, but just start. We've supplied you with the foundation to begin. Have fun with this new skill, get creative and build on your successes. Our intention is that someday all events will be inherently green. This truly is a journey, not a destination, and together we make a difference.

If all of this seems overwhelming, remember this: reduce first when and where you can, reuse second before buying new and as a last resort recycle.

Compelling Questions for Consideration:

1. How can the choices a meeting manager makes positively impact the community in which the event is being conducted?
2. How can you involve meeting attendees in the effort to have environmentally responsible meetings?
3. Name three ways to save money as well as the environment through green meeting practices.
4. What do you see as the competitive advantage of green meeting management for your organization?
5. Would you be able to sell the concept of green meetings to your clients?

We invite you to write us and share your successes, campfire stories and ideas at book@meetingstrategiesworldwide.com. We will share them with the rest of the green meeting planning community on our Web site.

Appendix

References

1. Meeting Strategies Worldwide. (2000). Conference data. Unpublished raw data.

2. Little, Amanda. (2005, May 10). It Was Just My Ecomagination, Grist Magazine. Retrieved April 18, 2006, from http://www.grist.org/news/muck/2005/05/10/little-ge/index.html

3. Environment Tops Priority List for Europe's Business Leaders. GreenBiz News. Retrieved February 21, 2007 from http://www.greenbiz.com/news/news_third.cfm?NewsID=34613

4. The Green Meetings Task Force, Convention Industry Council. (2004, April 6; Updated 2004, June 15). Green Meetings Report. Retrieved April 18, 2006, from http://www.conventionindustry.org/projects/green_meetings_report.pdf

5. Green Seal, Inc. (2002, April 19). Virginia Case Studies Report: Environmental Pollution Prevention Opportunity Assessments for the Hospitality Industry. Retrieved April 18, 2006, from http://www.deq.state.va.us/p2/lodging/pdf/report.pdf

6. Green Meeting Industry Council (2007). Greening the Hospitality Industry Conference. Unpublished raw data.

7. Meeting Strategies Worldwide. (2002). Greenbuild International Conference and Expo data. Unpublished raw data.

8. McPhee, M. (2006, September/October). A room with a very green view. In Business, 10-13.

9. Meeting Strategies Worldwide. (2004). Conference data. Unpublished raw data.

10. Object Class Analysis: Budget of the U.S. Government. Retrieved August 15, 2007, from http://www.whitehouse.gov/omb/budget/fy2008/pdf/objclass.pdf

11. The Moscone Center. (2007). Data collected by SMG/The Moscone Center.

12. Meeting Strategies Worldwide. (2006). Business for Social Responsibility Conference data. Unpublished raw data.

13. Energy Star – Compact Fluorescent Light Bulbs. Retrieved August 15, 2007, from http://www.energystar.gov/index.cfm?c=cfls.pr_cfls

14. United States Environmental Protection Agency. (2000). A Method for Quantifying Environmental Indicators of Select Leisure Activities in the United States. EPA-231-T-00-01.

15. WikiAnswers. Retrieved September 14, 2007, from http://wiki.answers.com/Q/What_are_the_dimensions_of_an_Olympic-sized_swimming_pool

16. Meeting Strategies Worldwide. (2005). Sierra Summit 2005 data. Raw unpublished data.

17. Meeting Strategies Worldwide. (2007). CB Richard Ellis conference data. Raw unpublished data.

18. APPENDIX C: Text of Emerson Good Samaritan Food Donation Act, PUBLIC LAW 104-210. (1990). Retrieved April 18, 2006, from http://www.usda.gov/news/pubs/gleaning/appc.htm

19. Monterey Bay Aquarium. Seafood Watch Guide, Frequently Asked Questions. Retrieved April 18, 2006, from http://www.mbayaq.org/cr/SeafoodWatch/web/sfw_faq.aspx

20. Environmental Defense Fund. (1998, June). An Ounce of Prevention: Think Before You Buy. EDF Letter, XXIX: 3, 7.

**Dollar to Euro exchange rate at time of printing is 1 USD:0.71 EUR

Resources

- America's Second Harvest – The Nation's Food Bank Network is the nation's largest charitable hunger-relief organization. http://www.secondharvest.org/

- Blue Ocean Institute – A mini-guide for environmentally responsible seafood choices. http://www.blueoceaninstitute.org

- Carbonfund – Offers carbon-offset opportunities. http://www.carbonfund.org

- Ceres Green Hotel Initiative – Tools to assist planners in selecting a green hotel. http://www.ceres.org/pub/publication.php?pid=61

- Chef's Collaborative – Website is for a national network of more than 1,000 members of the food community who promote sustainable cuisine. http://www.chefscollaborative.org/

- Climate Trust – This organization offers an online carbon-offset calculator. http://www.carboncounter.org/

- Convention Industry Council – A 30-member organization facilitates the exchange of information and develops programs to promote professionalism within the industry and educate the public. Green guidelines provided on Web site. http://www.conventionindustry.org/projects/green_meetings_report.pdf

- Consumers Union – Consumers Union, publishers of Consumer Reports, has a Web guide to environmental labels. http://www.eco-labels.org/home.cfm

- Earthware Biodegradables – Non-gmo wheat-based cutlery, corn-based cutlery, plates, cups, and more. http://www.earthwarebiodegradables.com

- EcoLogical Solutions – Assists hotels with economic and environmental savings. http://www.ecological-solutions.net

- Green Globe 21 – A worldwide benchmarking and certification program which facilitates sustainable travel and tourism for consumers, companies and communities. http://www.greenglobe21.com/

- Green Event Destinations Modeling Practice and Testing Markets – by Shawna McKinley, MA in Environmental Education and Communication Thesis, Royal Roads University – on resource page of the Meeting Strategies Worldwide's website http://www.meetingstrategiesworldwide.com

- Green Lodging News – Online newsletter
  http://www.greenlodgingnews.com
- Green Meeting Industry Council – Dedicated to promoting
  environmentally responsible practices within the meetings industry.
  http://www.greenmeetings.info
- Green Seal – Independent non-profit which provides several
  environmental standards plus eco-certification programs for products
  and hotels. http://www.greenseal.org
- IMEX – Co-sponsors Environmental Meeting Awards
  http://www.imex-frankfurt.com (Click on Vision Projects)
- Local Harvest – "Why Buy Local" – Describes the benefits of
  purchasing produce grown locally.
  http://www.localharvest.org/buylocal.jsp
- Meeting Strategies Worldwide – Case studies of environmentally
  responsible conferences and free resources.
  http://www.meetingstrategiesworldwide.com
- Monterey Bay Aquarium – Source for environmentally responsible
  seafood choices. http://www.mbayaq.org/cr/seafoodwatch.asp
- Oceans Alive – Part of the nonprofit Environmental Defense, the Web
  site includes what it calls the "Eco-Best" and "Eco-Worst" fish, as well as
  a downloadable, pocket-sized "Seafood Selector."
  http://www.oceansalive.org/eat.cfm
- Ocean's Blue Foundation: BlueGreen Meetings – Basic green meeting
  Web site for planners and suppliers. http://bluegreenmeetings.org
- Professional Convention Management Association (PCMA) Web site
  – Information about the Bill Emerson Good Samaritan Food Donation
  Act. http://www.pcma.org/source/community/network/usa/how/
  billemerson.asp
- Sustainable Travel International – Online newsletter -
  info@sustainabletravel.com
- Sustainable Travel Magazine – Bello Mundo
  http://www.bellomundo.com
- Terra Choice Environmental Services, Inc. – Organization dedicated
  to working with the marketplace to improve the environment by
  assisting organizations in turning their environmental challenges into
  opportunities. http://www.terrachoice.ca

- U.S. Dept. of Agriculture – The National Organic Program
  http://www.ams.usda.gov/nop/indexIE.htm
- U.S. Dept. of Agriculture: Food Recovery and Gleaning Initiative – This
  is a comprehensive guide to food donation laws, including links to state
  Good Samaritan Laws and resource lists and information on food
  recovery. http://www.usda.gov/news/pubs/gleaning/content.htm
- U.S. Environmental Protection Agency – Comprehensive manual on
  greening meetings.
  http://www.epa.gov/oppt/greenmeetings/
- World Centric – Fair Trade and Eco Store – Online store with several
  serviceware products that are biodegradable and compostable.
  http://www.worldcentric.org/store/index.htm
- Voluntourism online newsletter -
  http://www.voluntourism.org/newsletter.html
- *The Bottom Line of Green is Black* by Tedd Saunders, 1993*
- *The Consumer's Guide to Effective Environmental Choices* by Michael
  Brower and Warren Leon, Three Rivers Press, New York, 1999
- *The Ecology of Commerce* by Paul Hawken, 1993
- *Mid-Course Correction, Toward a Sustainable Enterprise: The Interface
  Model* by Ray Anderson, 1998*
- *Natural Capitalism: Creating the Next Industrial Revolution* by Paul
  Hawken, Amory Lovins and Hunter Lovins, 1999
- *The Natural Step for Business: Wealth, Ecology and the Evolutionary
  Corporation* by Brian Nattrass and Mary Altomare, 1999

*Book includes chapter on green meetings.

Glossary

APEX (Accepted Practices Exchange) – APEX is an initiative of the Convention Industry Council that is bringing together all stakeholders in the development and implementation of industry-wide accepted practices to create and enhance efficiencies throughout the meetings, conventions and exhibitions industry.

Biodegradable – Capable of being broken down by natural processes, such as bacterial action.

Biodiesel – A clean-burning, alternative fuel derived from animal fats or vegetable oil that can be used in diesel-burning engines. It does not contain petroleum products, but may be blended with petroleum-based diesel.

Carbon Offset – A way of counteracting the carbon emitted when the use of fossil fuel causes greenhouse gas emissions. Offsets commonly involve investing in projects such as renewable energy, tree-planting and energy-efficient projects.

Climate-Neutral – Products or services that reduce and offset the greenhouse gases generated at each stage of their life cycle on a cradle-to-cradle basis: the sourcing of their materials, their manufacturing or production, their distribution, use and ultimate end-of-life disposition.

Compost – A mixture of humus-rich, decomposed vegetable matter, used as a fertilizer or soil enrichment.

Ecological Footprint – The measure of area needed to supply national populations with the resources and area needed to absorb their wastes.

Ecology – The system of relationships between organisms and their environments.

Ecosystem – A community of living organisms interacting with themselves and with their environment.

Ecotourism – Tourism that respects the culture, natural history and environment of destinations and seeks to minimize the negative impact of travel on the environment.

Energy Star Equipment – A voluntary labeling program of the U.S. Environmental Protection Agency (EPA) and the U.S. Department of Energy that identifies energy-efficient products. Qualified products exceed minimum federal standards for energy consumption by a certain amount, or where no federal standards exist, have certain energy-saving features. Such products may display the Energy Star label.

Energy/Water Conservation – Practices and strategies that are designed to minimize the amount of energy and water used.

Environmentally Responsible Transportation – Transportation options that minimize environmental impact, such as mass public transportation (light rail, subway, electric/hybrid/biodiesel buses) and electric/hybrid vehicles.

Fair Trade – When small farmers are paid a fair market price that enables them to improve their standard of living.

Fossil Fuel – An organic, energy-rich substance formed from the long-buried remains of prehistoric life.

Green – A common expression meaning environmentally responsible.

Greenhouse Effect – Heating of the atmosphere that results from the absorption of solar radiation by certain gases.

Greenhouse Gas – A gas that contributes to the greenhouse effect by absorbing solar radiation. These gases include, but are not limited to, carbon dioxide, ozone, methane and chlorofluorocarbons.

Green Seal Certified – An organization, product or process that has passed a specific environmentally responsible standard as outlined by Green Seal.

Hybrid Vehicle – A vehicle that uses a combination of two engine types. Cars are most commonly gasoline-electric hybrids.

Kilowatt Hour – 1,000 watts of electricity used for one hour.

LEED – Leadership in Energy and Environmental Design – A Green Building Rating System® is a voluntary, consensus-based national standard for developing high-performance, sustainable buildings, developed by the U.S. Green Building Council.

Organic Foods – Grown without chemicals that can harm the land, water or human health. Organic certification of food can be through an independent organization or government program.

PDA – Personal digital assistant.

Pesticide – Any agent used to kill or control insects, weeds, rodents, fungi or other organisms.

Post-Consumer Material – An end product that has completed its life cycle as a consumer item and would otherwise have been disposed of as a solid waste. Post-consumer materials include recyclables collected in commercial and residential recycling programs, such as office paper, cardboard, aluminum cans, plastics and metals.

Post-Consumer Waste – Post-consumer waste is recycled material collected after people have tossed it in the recycle bin. Office recycling programs and household recycling programs are the main source of post-consumer waste.

Processed Chlorine Free (PCF) – "Processed chlorine free" describes a bleaching process free of chlorine or chlorine compounds, which poison rivers. The most common PCF bleaching agent is hydrogen peroxide (which breaks down into water and oxygen). Using PCF paper eliminates most of the toxic byproducts of traditional bleaching, such as dioxins and other organochlorides, and this means cleaner rivers.

Recycled Paper – According to U.S. government standards, uncoated paper with at least 30% post-consumer waste and coated paper with at least 10% post-consumer waste can be called "recycled" paper.

Recycling – The collection of waste materials and reprocessing them into new materials or products, which are then sold again.

Shade Grown Coffee – Coffee that is grown in the traditional manner, with coffee plants interspersed under a canopy of trees. End result: more habitats for birds, less need for chemical inputs, and the forest is not disrupted.

Trawling – Also known as dredging, the process of dragging huge, heavy nets over the sea floor, scooping up everything in their path.

Vegan – A lifestyle choice that excludes the consumption and use of animal flesh and by-products.

Vegetarian – A dietary choice that excludes the consumption of animal flesh or by-products, but may include eggs and dairy.

Vegetable-Based Inks – Environmentally friendly printing inks that are made from vegetable oils combined with pigments. The most common type is made from soy.

Venue – Location where an event takes place.

Volatile Organic Compounds (VOCs) – Compounds that have a high vapor pressure and low water solubility. Many VOCs are human-made chemicals used and produced in the manufacture of paints, pharmaceuticals and refrigerants. VOCs typically are industrial solvents, such as trichloroethylene; fuel oxygenates, such as methyl tert-butyl ether (MTBE); or by-products produced by chlorination in water treatment, such as chloroform. VOCs are often components of petroleum fuels, hydraulic fluids, paint thinners and dry cleaning agents. VOCs are common groundwater contaminants.

About Us –
Meeting Strategies Worldwide

Based in Portland, Oregon, in the United States, Meeting Strategies Worldwide provides conference management, consulting and training services to a diverse clientele. Recognized internationally as the leaders in developing and implementing innovative, state-of-the-art green meeting strategies, we have created the premier line of green meeting resources known as MeetGreen^{SM}. This suite of resources and tools includes the MeetGreen^{SM} Calculator, the industry's first and foremost measurement tool for assessing the environmental impact of events, and the MeetGreen^{SM} Certification process, the only industry program for validating green meeting practices and outcomes.

As a result of our commitment to the environment, Meeting Strategies Worldwide and its clients have been awarded the prestigious IMEX Green Meetings Award four times since its inception. This award is the highest international accolade of its kind.

Business principals Amy Spatrisano, CMP, and Nancy J. Wilson, CMP, are founding board members of the Green Meeting Industry Council, a nonprofit group that promotes environmental stewardship and green meeting practices in the meetings and hospitality industries. Amy and Nancy wrote the Green Guidelines for the Live Earth concert series and served on the Live Earth Green Team, charged with greening the Giants Stadium venue. Amy spearheaded and chaired the Green Task Force for the Convention Industry Council (CIC), which produced the Green Meeting Report. Together, Nancy and Amy authored the chapter on green meetings for the *Professional Convention Management Association's book, Professional Meeting Management: Comprehensive Strategies for Meetings, Conventions and Events (5th Ed.).*

Both Nancy and Amy have spoken at numerous local, national and international hospitality meetings and conferences on the topic of green meetings, helping to educate meeting planners and suppliers on practices that reduce waste, support local economies and minimize environmental impact.

Amy Spatrisano, CMP and Nancy J. Wilson, CMP
Principals of Meeting Strategies Worldwide, Inc.

Get started today!

For more information and resources on green
meetings and events, visit us at:
www.meetingstrategiesworldwide.com
www.meetgreen.com

Meeting Strategies Worldwide offers:
- Training seminars
- Strategic environmental consulting
- Comprehensive conference management
- Customized training programs
- Green checklists and tools
- Free quarterly newsletter